"Some say Allbright is a magnetic mixture of Mark Twain and Garrison Keillor, but he has his own blend of Southern humor, charm, and witty magic."
Columbia State-Record

"There's a gentle amusement in the stories Allbright tells. He's watching and chuckling not *at* people but with them."
Baton Rouge Sunday Magazine

"He has timing, a delicate touch, an exquisite sense of the foibles of human nature. He has the guts to consider sadness, fallibility and mortality, and the skill to make his considerations ring true."
Jack Butler

"Allbright can't help committing literature, and is the only writer I know of who uses the editorial 'we' without sounding like Haile Selassie. His column is like that mythical jungle watering hole, where wild beasts pull in their claws and savages lay down their spears...It is often the only thing in the paper that reminds us that we are one people, or even one species."
Mike Trimble, Arkansas Times

"Charles Allbright has a fine comic touch like no one else I know. Day after day he's funny, and I don't know how he does it."
Charles Portis

GravelyThe Mules Stopped Dancing

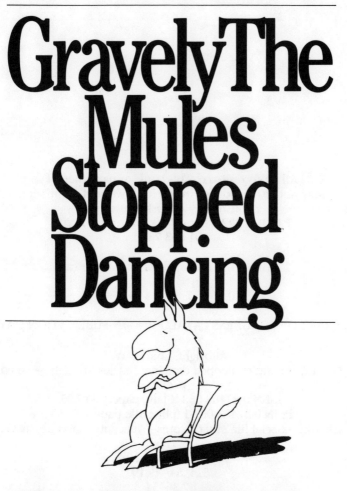

Humor By
Charles Allbright

August House / Little Rock
PUBLISHERS

Published by August House, Inc.,
P.O. Box 3223, Little Rock, Arkansas, 72203,
501-663-7300.

Printed in the United States of America

10 9 8 7 6 5 4 3 2 1

LIBRARY OF CONGRESS CATALOGING-IN-PUBLICATION DATA

Allbright, Charles W.
Gravely the mules stopped dancing/Charles Allbright.—1st ed.
p. cm.
ISBN 0-87483-063-X (alk. paper): $19.95.
ISBN 0-87483-062-1 (pbk.: alk. paper): $8.95
1. Arkansas—Social life and customs—Anecdotes, facetiae, satire, etc.
I. Title.
PN4874.A37G7 1988
814'.54—dc19
87-36454
CIP

First Edition, 1988

Cover illustration by Bill Jennings
Production artwork by Ira Hocut
Typography by Lettergraphics
Design direction by Ted Parkhurst
Project direction by Hope Coulter

For my mother and father

Contents

Stand Back for a Stampede of Fools   *11*
Our Diary Is Around Here Somewhere   *33*
Your Average Bachelor Does Not Understand This   *69*
Would They Come and Find Him Slightly Ajar?   *87*
Breakfasts of Friskies and Meow Mix   *103*
Dancing His Dance for Some Other Crowd   *121*
Hearing Things We Never Heard Before   *137*
Somebody Will Forgive a Father's Gulping   *153*

The incident for which this book is named
has not yet occurred.

Charles Allbright

Stand Back for a Stampede of Fools

Modern Moviegoers More in the Dark than Ever

When the film broke in one of the theaters at Breckenridge Village's Cinema City the other evening, a prolonged period of unease set in.

Nobody in the seats knew what to do. Apparently nobody in the projection booth knew what to do.

"What is this?" a voice said vaguely from the seats.

They had been watching *Trading Places* when everything flashed away. The screen went blank.

The voice—"What is this?"—could have come from a pygmy looking at a Zippo cigarette lighter.

"Beats me," says the associate pygmy, while everybody else ties Frank Buck to the stake.

The moment of the film breakdown was a strange thing to be a part of, according to our correspondent on the scene.

"The movie must have been off for a full ten minutes," she reports. "I got the distinct impression that nobody in the theater had ever seen a film break before."

There is a marked difference between the personalities of motion picture fans who pay four dollars a seat and those who used to get in for a dime.

"You have to raise a little Cain"—that's how our correspondent put it.

She was recalling Cain raised by patrons of the old Ritz Theater in Russellville. The Ritz and the Lowery.

Back then the film broke all the time. Broke and ran away, throwing flapping noises through the hole in the projection booth.

As fast as he could, the projectionist got his apology on the screen: ONE MOMENT PLEASE.

It made no particle of difference. Nobody wondered, "What is this?"

"When the film broke, the place went crazy. Everybody whistled and clapped, and the boys stomped their feet."

The girls did not stomp their feet.

"They said there were rats in there, looking for popcorn. I never actually saw any rats, but I never took my feet out of the seat, either."

It was not what you would call *modern slick,* that apology plastered up there, tilted, on the screen.

"It was typed on this narrow strip of paper, like it might have come out of a fortune cookie."

In his torment, the projectionist just as often got the wrong idea up there, something left over from the previous Saturday afternoon: Johnny Coleman Your Mother Says Come Home.

Or maybe he threw up "Fri. Sat. Sun."

Our correspondent explains, "'Fri. Sat. Sun' was supposed to be superimposed on a coming attraction." On the suddenly blank screen, it drew more hoots than ONE MOMENT PLEASE, but not as many as Johnny Coleman.

At Cinema City, when *Trading Places* disappeared, those in the audience had nothing to look at.

"They didn't even have tadpoles."

Tadpoles were trash on the old projector lens. On the blank screen they wiggled, blown by the fan that cooled the equipment. Most tadpoles could not maintain their hold. They vanished abruptly, fleeing toward the high ceiling of the Ritz or the Lowery.

Only a fool would contend that a dime bought more than four dollars buys.

Stand back for a stampede of fools.

The last projection booth message we saw on a picture show screen was on a narrow strip of yellow paper, thrown up there at an angle, then jerked back and reinserted more or less properly.

This was in the New Theater, near Markham and Main in Little Rock.

What the booth operator managed to get up there that

13

afternoon was this:

"Americans Bombed at Pearl Harb."

Wherever Pearl Harb was, we didn't stay around looking for tadpoles.

Charlie Allbright, your mother says come home.

Projection Room Breakdown a Bargain at Any Price

This comes from Fred Barlow of near Batesville:

"The column about film breakage, and anxiety in the projection booth, reminded me of a particular bargain everyone enjoyed one afternoon in the old Royal Theater on Main Street in Little Rock.

"I say everyone enjoyed it. In fact, there was a long storm of howling and catcalls, which frightened me as a country boy visitor. But I enjoyed the bargain."

The bargain was that the afternoon's feature, a single attraction, started out with Sonja Henie and wound up in a jungle stampede.

Fred Barlow recalls:

"We had gone to see the skating picture. In the moment before the film broke, Sonja Henie was gliding across the ice to the strains of some now-forgotten romantic ballad."

Suddenly the film broke—flap, flap—"ONE MOMENT PLEASE!"

"When the picture came back on, Miss Henie was nowhere to be seen. Instead, terrified savages were being chased out of a jungle by about one thousand elephants."

The man in the Royal projection booth never got things straightened out.

After almost fifty years, Barlow concludes, "I'll never find out what happened to Sonja, or *why* that happened to the savages, but it was the biggest picture show bargain I ever got in to."

Back home in Independence County, Freddy Barlow was a hero for many days.

He explained to his friends, "But I wouldn't do it again, because those people who go to the show in Little Rock are crazy."

Our man Leland DuVall recalls picture shows as they

15

came to the Moreland community, north of Russellville.

That was back before pictures talked. The Moreland showing was a sometimes thing.

"Our night was Wednesday night," DuVall says.

The traveling picture show man was equipped with a hand-cranked projector, borne about in a Model T truck.

"This thing was illuminated by what they called an ether vapor lamp. I can believe it, from the way the thing smelled."

The ether lamp had to be lighted outside, in a ceremony conducted as dusk drew near.

"Stand back, boys," the picture show man said. "And don't anybody smoke."

Everybody stood back. As many came to see the lighting of the ether lamp as came to see the picture show. It was all included in the dime.

"That was good advice about standing back," DuVall says. "One slip and the whole thing would have gone up."

So with the ether lamp lighted, and dark at hand, everybody bought a ten-cent ticket and followed the lamp into the theater.

Actually, it wasn't a theater.

"It was an old empty store. Today I guess it would be called a community center."

Here was where the Moreland team played its basketball. There were posts in there, and a low ceiling, both factors in Moreland's permanent game plan, and nightmarish for any visiting basketball team.

For the Wednesday night picture show, ticket holders sat on planks that rested on barrels. You didn't want to get behind a post.

Leland DuVall remembers the night the traveling picture show man got sick and sent somebody in his place to run the fancy projector.

"The picture was a shoot-'em-up, of course."

With everybody in place on the benches, whiffing ether, the substitute man started cranking.

"I believe in that first scene people were walking in reverse away from the train station. The train itself was backing off down the track, with smoke coming out of the air and shooting down into the smokestack."

The substitute man stopped cranking. He worked a long time getting everything straightened out.

The picture show began again.

"This time one man on horseback was chasing a gang of about twenty, and they were all galloping backwards. There was a lot of gunfire, with puffs of smoke going back into the pistol barrels."

Somebody shouted from out of the ether fumes, "Hold those ticket stubs!"

DuVall recalls, "We got to see the picture the next Wednesday, with all the smoke going the right way."

It was one of the great bargains in motion picture history.

"Hit and Run" Has New Meaning for Blindfolded Driver

Joe Marsh of Pine Bluff refreshes our memory about hometown excitement, back in the days when entertainment was entertainment.

"You forgot to mention," Marsh says, "that the same fellow who brought the tent picture show to town also put on a show of driving down Main Street blindfolded."

Back then people had talent.

"I saw a man drive from one end of Dumas to the other with his shirt tied around his face. I know he couldn't see because before starting this amazing drive he sat there in the auto seat and passed his hand back and forth in front of his eyes, shaking his head."

The amazing drive had a breathtaking climax.

"Right at the end, an unsuspecting woman walked in front of the car and was struck sprawling. The blindfolded motorist had slowed to about two miles an hour."

As onlookers gasped, the woman scrambled to her feet and began caning the unseeing driver. Or, she umbrellaed him.

"She whomped until the crowd pulled her off. It was a very exciting moment, proving that the driver hadn't cheated and peeped."

Later, Joe Marsh was amazed to hear that the same unsuspecting woman was struck by the same blindfolded driver down the highway in McGehee.

"I understand a similar accident happened also at Dermott, and later at Lake Village. They kept showing up in the same towns together."

People couldn't figure how the woman kept making so many narrow escapes.

Joe Marsh recalls, "I felt sorrier for the guy who kept getting hit with the umbrella."

A Little Rock reader, who grew up in a small town, recalls those old traveling tent show days.

"Admission was very low, ten cents or so. The show owner would accept milk, butter, or garden vegetables. One boy, whose family had none of these things, was resourceful enough to buy a dozen eggs at a store where his family had credit and sell them at a store down the street for a dime to get money for the show."

Not everybody could come up with the dime.

"Some boys, with no hope of getting in honestly, crawled under the tent, with help from friends inside. One especially harsh show owner went around the inside of the tent, hitting fingers, hands, and sometimes heads of boys attempting to lift the edge of the tent and crawl in free.

"He would not get by now with that—he would have some lawsuits on his hands. But back then boys had never heard of their 'rights,' and if caught in some misdoing simply took their lumps cheerfully."

She remembers the time, this reader does, when her big city cousin from Conway came to visit.

"Anxious to show him that we, too, had entertainment, we took him to a tent show, which luckily was in town. This show had three reels. The first reel went okay. The showman then changd reels, as the crowd waited. In the second reel the cowboy got the girl and they rode off into the sunset."

Everybody got up to leave.

The traveling show owner shouted, "Wait! Wait! I made a mistake. I showed the last reel instead of the second reel."

Everybody sat down again, then watched the middle reel to its nonconclusion.

It is not known what the city cousin from Conway thought about the plot of this western.

Yes, people back then had talent.

"One showman, a Mr. Hicks, said he could read

minds. He also could hypnotize people, he said. Some boys went up as subjects for this demonstration and did act like a dog, cat, donkey, or other animal on command. Maybe it was agreed they do this in return for a free admission. Who knows?"

Mr. Hicks also was an outstanding blindfolded driver. With a volunteer beside him, a teacher, he got into the car and started out blindfolded by a heavy towel, held in place with adhesive tape.

"They crossed the railroad and Hicks almost ran into a ditch. He fussed at his guide. Said she wasn't keeping her mind on what she was to think about."

Depression Youth Had a Hot Time in Show Business

MALVERN.—In the tenderness of his teens, Charles Roark left Malvern for the hot lights of show business. The hot lights and the high living.

It was the time of the Great Depression. Show business was a traveling tent show.

Charles Roark, youthful magician and ventriloquist whiz, took second billing only to Professor Roberts, owner of the traveling show.

Well, to Professor Roberts and to Ted the Wonder Dog.

"Also," says Roark, "I made the candy pitch. 'Golden Nuggets' candy kisses, with a prize in each and every package."

In the dog days of another summer, a half-century later, the young performer of yesteryear is put to remembering.

"We played small towns, mostly on dirt roads, towns too small to have a local theater. The stay was a week to ten days."

The advertising was smashing.

"The main means was to go to the telephone office, usually in the front room of some woman's house. We gave Central a family pass for the entire engagement. For this she rang the party line and got everybody in the area on the phone to announce the show was in town.

"If the town was big enough to have a sidewalk, we mixed lime and water and painted the sidewalk with advertising."

Getting there was half the fun.

"The troupe consisted of Professor Roberts and his sons and me. Once we made a long jump, about forty miles over gravel roads, with no spare tire. We had a flat about every fifteen minutes, all day long."

Too late, the tent show pulled into town.

"We started erecting the tent anyway, and hired a little boy to help us, promising him a pass for his work. Along about suppertime he informed us that he had to go home and eat."

The stars of the hot lights had no money.

"The only thing we had to eat was a jar of huckleberry jam that someone had given us the night before instead of money. We had plenty of prize candy, Golden Nuggets, but I never heard of anyone in the show biz getting hungry enough to eat any of that."

Charles Roark went to work.

"I sat the kid down on the front row, got on stage, and made the greatest candy pitch of my life. I said if he'd go home and bring us a pan of hot biscuits, I'd give him five free boxes. We dined that night on jam and hot biscuits."

The feature film was *Birth of a Nation,* twelve reels with twelve records, each about three feet wide, to provide the sound.

"One of Professor Roberts's sons, Herman, was the operator. He liked to read Zane Grey novels while the picture was showing, so he usually got the wrong record on.

"While Lillian Gish and Henry B. Walthal were doing the love scenes, you could hear battle sounds of the Civil War. When the battle was raging, 'Love's Old Sweet Song' played in the background."

There was a single critical moment.

"The third reel showed the assassination of Lincoln in Ford's Theater. There was a close-up of Booth's hand with the pistol, and when he fired there was a puff of smoke out of the barrel."

When Herman Roberts got the record to "bang!" anywhere close to that puff, that was a successful night.

Yes, that was hot entertainment, all right.

"In those days film was made of celluloid and was highly flammable.

"One night the belt on the take-up reel broke and ran

about one thousand feet of film out on the floor. Herman was reading the Zane Grey book and failed to notice it until he threw his cigarette on the pile of film. It burned the whole tent down."

They rebuilt the show—it must go on—and continued the dusty road tour.

But not Charles Roark.

"I had to leave the show to return to Malvern and go to high school. This was a chapter of show biz that only a few people remember. It brought entertainment to rural areas where the nearest picture show was often fifty miles away."

Whale Expert Recalls His Days with "Colossus!"

MALVERN.—They called themselves the Pacific Coast Whaling Company.

What they had was one old whale, embalmed to the gills, mounted on a railroad flatcar.

In everlasting repose, the whale had his mouth propped wide open.

Charles Roark once slept in that cavernous mouth.

He recalls, "The whale was just a tremendous attraction."

Roark at 64 is retired at Malvern, the hometown he left as a teenager to go with a traveling tent picture show.

In half a century the man traveled with seventeen circus groups, Ringling among them, performing Punch and Judy in the sideshow and an illusion act in center ring.

When circuses went to Florida for the winter, Roark hooked up with medicine shows and burlesque companies.

And, glory be, with "Colossus!" the whale.

"I remember the day I joined the show in Valdosta, Georgia. I didn't have to ask anybody where the whale was showing. I just followed my nose. I suppose the human body can get used to anything. It wasn't but a few days until I was able to sit on the whale and eat my lunch."

Charles Roark became a lecturer for the Pacific Coast Whaling Company.

"They gave me a seaman's uniform with gold braid and a stick to point with."

And they provided a lecture to memorize.

"I wasn't allowed to use any sideshow imagination. The lecture was in case somebody visited the attraction who might really know something about a whale."

His lecture memorized, Roark became an authority on the gape-mouthed "Colossus!"

The show employed nothing but authorities.

24

"I recall one old carney, he was known to us as 'Whale Oil Gus,' and his job was to go a day ahead of the show and lecture to the schoolchildren to whet their appetite to see the big whale. He had done it so long and so well that he actually believed he was a sea captain."

And come they did, Depression days children of all ages, wide-eyed and grabbing their noses.

"The whale was just about as long as the railroad car. We had a man whose job it was to go around the whale searching for soft spots and putting in more embalming fluid."

Local folks lined up at both ends of the car, paid dimes, and came aboard.

"If I was lecturing at the tail, another expert would be walking around in his uniform, pointing and lecturing at the whale's head. The people just kept coming, it was tremendous, the line never stopping."

Except right at the end.

"At the exit we had an expert who picked up a lump of something and called it ambergris. He explained that ambergris was an ingredient produced by the whale, highly valuable because it was converted into exotic perfume. We just happened to have plenty of that exotic perfume available right there on the railroad car for fifteen cents a bottle."

In combination, old "Colossus!" and the fifteen-cent perfume created an eye-watering atmosphere.

Nor was that all.

As an added attraction the Pacific Coast Whaling Company displayed a mermaid. Well mummified.

"What it was," Charles Roark says, "was half-monkey and half-fish. Somehow they managed to get the top of this monkey, his arms and head and everything, attached to the bottom of a fish."

There was no extra charge for seeing the mermaid.

That night in the whale's mouth?

"We got to a small town in inland Florida. The deal was that we bought tickets in the chair car and for that they let us pull the whale along behind the rest of the train."

Reaching town, the whale car was uncoupled on a sidetrack.

"That night it was too late to get a room without waking somebody up. I just made a pallet with some curtains we had there and slept in the whale's mouth like Jonah."

Remember the Whale that Came to Town?

At Fort Smith, Mrs. Eugene Gaston wanted to roll the newspaper up and hit her daughter across the face with it.

"I *told* you I saw a whale at the railroad station when I was a little girl!"

But Mrs. Gaston's daughter has a daughter of her own.

"I couldn't hit her in front of my granddaughter, but I sure made her read about the whale that came through town during the Depression.

"Hooray! Hooray for all of us who never convinced our darling children."

"Relieved" is the word used by a reader at North Little Rock. Back in those days she was a youngster at Stuttgart.

"I was beginning to believe I never saw the whale, that maybe I just made the whole thing up."

The aroma of tea has caused the problem. Freshly brewed hot tea.

"I associate that smell with the smell at that railroad car."

Over the years she said, "Whew. This tea smells like a dead whale."

And they always said, with increasing derision, "Aw, when did you ever smell a dead whale?"

If somebody had been handy last week, she would have whapped them with a rolled-up newspaper.

When she was six or seven, Nancy Weinberger went to see an embalmed whale sidetracked on a flatcar in east Little Rock.

"What the whole end of town smelled like was not to be believed, and people all around there were eating popcorn and peanuts!"

Young Nancy worked up a cry, not difficult under the circumstances, until her father bought a tiny red Bible,

27

one of the whale items on sale, along with popcorn, peanuts, and exotic perfume.

"I didn't read the Bible, maybe I didn't even open it until I was about twelve."

What the whale folks sold her father was a book of Jonah.

Hubert McDonald says that the subject should not be scuttled without a mention of the headless woman who traveled with "Colossus!" the whale.

Not everybody saw the headless woman because she didn't appear at every showing, having other chores to perform.

"She sat up there in that special chair, with all those wires coming out of her neck, or appearing to, moving her arms and legs. I believe the headless woman was the wife of the fellow who was running things."

On other days the crowd made do with "Colossus!" and the mermaid, a mummified monkey torso rigged up to a fish tail.

The mermaid was not capable of movement, which was probably just as well.

When she was a youngster in Palahatchee, Mississippi, not far from Jackson, Dorothy Webber Grissom's family joined the throng to view a huge whale on a flatcar.

Mrs. Grissom recalls it now from Malvern.

"Several days after the viewing Mama baked a big fish whole. It must have been a foot or more in length and was a beautiful thing as it reposed on the platter.

"We sat down to dinner, the six of us, all quiet, mouths watering, all eyes admiring the baked fish. Suddenly young Bud spoke out loud and clear, 'That fish smells just like that old whale!'"

The beautiful fish got thrown out.

Ewing Kinkead also saw that dead whale.

"Back in those days on Saturday morning I always went to Seventh and Rock Streets for my violin lesson.

Afterward I had a nickel for candy at the dime store, and a dime to go to the New Theater up on Main Street where the bus station is now."

Kinkead had finished his music lesson one Saturday and was working on the candy, en route to the picture show, when he passed an open doorfront between Third and Second Streets on Main.

That was before air conditioning, and something powerful was inside the building.

"They said it was formaldehyde you were smelling, but I think it was mostly whale."

There was no way for a boy in his early teens not to go in.

"The whale got my dime that day, and I definitely got the full effect of it."

The effect lingered long after the picture show was over.

What Does One Do with Six Embalmed Whales?

You can keep an embalmed whale around only so long. Beyond that the whale is no longer an asset.

It was a close thing even to begin with.

So what finally happens to the whale?

What does an owner do, in fact, with six embalmed whales whose show business days on railroad flatcars are over?

H.H. McDonald of North Little Rock knows the answer.

McDonald's cousin, Lucille Savage, married a New Yorker named Hutton who traveled the country exhibiting a whale and selling exotic perfume said to be made from the whale's ambergris.

Those were the hungering years of the 1930s.

"That first whale was so profitable," McDonald recalls, "they wound up buying six whales and sending the attraction in all directions."

At all stops folks lined up to pay a dime and see the whale, and buy exotic perfume for fifteen cents a bottle.

Hutton took his whales to England.

It was over there that the cultural attraction choked on its own environment.

"They were going around everywhere looking for enough formaldehyde to keep putting in the whales."

At last Hutton hired a tugboat.

"They pulled the whales out to sea, about fifty or sixty miles off the English coast.

"And then they blew the whales up. Exploded them with dynamite. It was a matter of getting everything separated."

The war was coming on.

It would have been interesting to read any coded alarm flashed home by a U-boat captain.

And the resulting communiqué—"They're doing

what? *Dummkopf!* Return immediately to the Father-
land!"

So Hutton came back to the United States without his
cultural attraction.

It was only temporary.

Cousin-in-law H.H. McDonald says, "The man had
always been in some kind of show business and he didn't
stay out of it long."

Hutton bought one of the last large Chevrolet trucks
available before the war.

"He modified the truck. He put some steps leading up
to the bed and built an observation platform so people
could walk around up there."

To observe what?

"He went over to Lebanon, Tennessee, and bought
this huge hog. I've seen the hog's name in the records. His
name was Superba Wave and he weighed twelve hundred
pounds. I believe Hutton paid five hundred dollars for
him."

So the Huttons set out with their newest attraction, the
"World's Largest Hog!"—having added, in McDonald's
recollection, about 500 pounds to the original weight.

"Hutton didn't ride with the hog. He never touched it.
They rode along in a Cadillac. There was another man to
drive and manage the hog, or maybe two men."

The hog was a whale of an attraction.

"I remember seeing him when they came through
North Little Rock. It was at a feed store at Washington and
Poplar."

For two days people lined up with their dimes to climb
the steps and walk around in there looking at the "World's
Largest Hog!"

"Wherever they went the hog took in between two
hundred and two hundred-fifty dollars a day."

And ate how much?

"Lord I don't know."

For the rest of his life Superba Wave, accompanied by
the Cadillac, traveled the countryside. It is not clear
whether he produced ambergris.

Our Diary Is Around Here Somewhere

"Magnificant" Recollections from "My Diary"

At an odds and ends store in western Little Rock, Mrs. Don Singleton overheard a customer ask about a diary.

The sales clerk could not have been more than eighteen. She said, "A what please?"

The customer said, "A diary. A personal journal."

The young clerk appeared mystified, and then—"Oh, yes. I mean, no. We had one of those around here for the longest time. Nobody bought it and I think somebody here in the store finally took it home."

Sarah Singleton wants to know: "Whatever happened to everyone's diary? None of us back in Forrest City could have grown up without one."

Our diary is around here somewhere.

The last time we saw the diary its gold snap had turned green and wouldn't stay in its fool-proof locking place. That was some years ago. Forty or so.

The diary was called "My Diary." At first we thought it had something to do with milk cows.

"It's for your personal thoughts," an uncle explained.

Like what thoughts?

He said, "Well, that's up to you. Like the things you do and think, but you want to keep them private."

We went off and sat down with the small red book and thought about personal thoughts.

Was he kidding? A person would have to be a fool.

So we wrote movie reviews in "My Diary."

"Tonight was the best picture show there ever was. It was *Gunga Din.* There never has been any other show half as good. Alton laughed when Gunga got shot and played wrong notes on the bugle and fell off of the steeple. I will never forget *Gunga Din.* Alton is my worst friend."

We didn't speak to Alton for a week. Or at least during the whole next morning.

An uncle gives a person a diary and that person appreciates it, even if he can't write down personal thoughts. What if somebody found the key? Or just tore the fool-proof lock off?

So:

"Tonight was the best picture show ever made. It was *On Borrowed Time*. When she was about to die she was knitting, and death came down out of the apple tree and said to her, 'You're tapering off now.' I am sorry for crying on the paper. I will never forget *On Borrowed Time*. It was magnificant."

In the summer we saw our uncle again.

"How's the diary?" he said.

We told him the diary was fine.

"Do you write in it a lot?"

We said yes.

"That's good."

Not once did he ask what got said in "My Diary." We never told him.

"Tonight was the best picture show of all time. It was *Santa Fe Trail*. It had Errol Flynn and Ronald Reagan. Raymond Massey was John Brown. He said as God is my witness he would be back. They hanged Raymond at Harper's Ferry. Errol got Olivia DeHavilland but Ronald didn't care, and they were happy. I will never forget *Santa Fe Trail*."

A diary entry about *One in a Million*, the greatest picture show ever made, was torn out. That was the show after which, at age nine, we decided to marry Sonja Henie, with those dimples and little niblet teeth, and all that running around on the toes of her skates. The entry was destroyed because we were already spoken for by an older girl next door, Mary Ella Ward, although she did not know it at the time.

There were other picture shows that we will never forget, but they do not come to mind offhand.

And now the record, "My Diary," seems to have been misplaced. It was right here somewhere, not more than forty or so years ago.

35

Pool Hall the Same after All These Years

When Bill Stroud, a Philadelphia newspaperman, came down to McGehee to cover that city's "Railroad Days," he took a sentimental walk along Railroad Street.

Bill Stroud grew up at McGehee.

His brothers, George and Joe, also are newspapermen, at St. Louis and Detroit. They would have understood his stroll.

The Strouds were properly sheltered through boyhood, as were other newspaper people who came out of that same town.

Not one of them, that we know of, ever actually set foot inside the pool hall on Railroad Street.

All longed to.

To begin with, inside the pool hall were real men. They walked around these long tables, chalking their cues, shooting actual pool.

In the foreground at smaller tables sat men playing dominoes. They made those ivories clack.

From the sidewalk outside, a sensitive person could feel the clacking through his nose, flattened against the front window.

We cannot speak for the Strouds, but at our own house the most daring thing ever done at a table, besides eating, was playing a rousing round of Rook.

And those cards were put away at sundown on Saturday.

Even marbles were not played for "keeps." "Keeps" was a form of gambling, which was not permitted in better homes.

Author cards were permitted.

"Give me all your Ralph Waldo Emersons."

This was before anybody could read.

"Is Ralph Waldo the one with the mustache?"

36

All the great writers had abundant facial hair, except for Amy Russell Lowell. But after a few grubby hands, you could not be certain about even her.

Regular Monopoly was not permitted. Dice were not rolled under our roof.

Open the Bible and close your eyes and put your finger down on, say, the 23rd Psalm. Move forward 23 spaces to Marvin Gardens. As wonderful as this was as a form of Christian teaching, the game lacked something. Especially when most of the money was being stolen while the player's eyes were closed.

So, of course, marbles never were played for keeps. And yet on occasion a third-grader would come home without the marbles he took that day to school. Usually he had run into Curtis Hornor Jr.

Grave parental discussion ensued.

"Charles says he needs a nickel for a tablet."

"A tablet? Son, I thought you bought a new tablet just yesterday."

Yessir, well, there was an explanation for that. We had been writing a lot, thinking about becoming one of the great authors like Henry Wadsworth or Longfellow. We were even starting to grow a beard so, you see, the new tablet was all written up.

"Son, let's see your knuckles."

If there is one thing a great author can't hide, it is grimy hands, with a colossal callus adorning the bottom knuckle of his middle shooting finger.

"Where are your marbles?"

Marbles? Oh. What happened was, we got a hole in our pocket and all our marbles fell out.

Pulled wrongside-out, the pocket somehow had mended itself.

"Charles, have you been playing keeps?"

Keeps! If that's what anybody thought, if that's all the faith anybody had—well! They could just forget the whole thing, the tablet, the literary career—see if we grew a beard! Just forget it!

"All right, son. And while you're at it, let's just forget

supper, too."

We wondered what Curtis Hornor Jr. told his folks about where he found all his new marbles.

But about that pool hall. There was one other thing.

Somewhere inside the pool hall on Railroad Street was said to be a picture magazine called *Sunshine and Health*. In this magazine people were said to take off everything but their shoes and play volleyball.

If we ever saw *Sunshine and Health* through the window of the pool hall, we never made it out. Everything in there, seen through the tunnel formed by cupping one's palms to one's eyes—everything in there looked far away and under water.

So when Bill Stroud got to the pool hall, on his sentimental walk along Railroad Street, he put his hand on the door and opened it.

It is not clear whether Stroud actually stepped inside, only that after all these years he wanted a view not obstructed by amber window glass, to see what changes two decades had wrought.

His pupils required some adjusting. From pinpoints in the glaring sun, they widened gradually until things took shape before him.

Stroud described it to us later:

"I don't think anybody had moved. I know nobody had left. It was like somebody had locked the door, stopping everything back there in 1959. And I was the first one to open it."

Beware, Children, of the Pool Hall

At Heber Springs, Mrs. B.B. Munson and some other women of the church served Sunday dinner to a visiting preacher and his family.

During the meal everybody said how good the morning sermon was.

The preacher said he just didn't know.

The world was getting crazier every day.

Young folks, especially, were not learning the important lessons they used to.

"When I was a boy I was scared to death of a pool hall. I wouldn't go within a hundred yards of a pool hall."

One of the ladies said, "Yes, and it made you a better man, didn't it."

The preacher said of course it made him a better man.

At least he thought it had.

Although to tell the truth he wasn't certain at all.

"Actually I didn't know what a pool hall was. I knew they played dominoes in there, whatever dominoes were."

But that wasn't the worst.

"What kept me scared away was I thought if you went inside the pool hall you had to get naked and jump in the pool."

We have a nostalgic pool hall note from Sue Zan Mizell of North Little Rock.

Not that she ever went inside one of the things.

"Being the baby girl of an extremely conservative preacher in Gurdon twenty-five years ago, I passed by the pool hall day after day and gazed with fascination and intrigue into that dimly-lit den of iniquity.

"There was a padlock (unlatched while the business was open) on a pivot-type hinge that fit across the two front doors. Every time I passed and saw that lock, a little dickens would tell me to lock it. I managed to resist for quite some time, but eventually succumbed to the little voice."

Later Sue Zan's older brother told her there was no back door to the place.

"Dominoes was the only worldly game my father would play, and I could not really understand why it was wrong inside those walls."

At any rate, she did the Christian thing and locked the players up in there.

That was a long time ago.

"The pool hall is gone now. My dad is in Heaven, and I wouldn't venture to guess as to where the men who were in that establishment are."

Some people were talking about old-timey pool halls, and how no self-respecting young person ever saw the inside of one, except when he ran through there on a dare. And then he ran mostly with his eyes closed.

But Nelle Phelan said, shoot, back then she knew all about pool halls.

Well, not all about them.

As a youngster growing up at Durant, Mississippi, Nelle Phelan went to the pool hall on a regular basis.

Regularly, once a year.

That was on Armistice Day, or Veterans Day, or Poppy Day. Whatever.

On that special day young girls called at American Legion headquarters and got their supplies of paper poppies. Then they went out on the streets and sold them.

But not Nelle Phelan.

She lit a shuck for the pool hall.

Eddie Phelan tells about his wife's resourcefulness as a youngster.

"She made a killing. Everybody in that pool hall bought a poppy, and they all paid good prices for them. Nelle was the prize poppy salesman in town."

Actually she didn't learn a great deal about the inside workings of a pool hall.

Selling poppies in there was pretty much like running through on a dare. You did it mostly with your eyes closed.

A Gawl Stone Record?

Professor James E. Griner of Arkansas State University, to whom we are indebted for several large disclosures, has reason to believe he has done it again.

"I have neglected you for some period of time," Professor Griner writes, "and therefore feel compelled to inform you of the latest news in Jonesboro—to wit:

"A woman here in Jonesboro recently had her gall bladder removed and there were 64 stones in it. The husband believes this is a record, although so far as I know he has not informed that fellow Guinness.

"P.S. I did say 64. That's what the husband told me. I did not count them, or have a chance to do so."

It is not yet time to call in Guinness.

We had an uncle once who took out his own gallstones. He was not really our uncle, except that he was everybody's "Uncle," a man of (in retrospect) indeterminate age and association, who showed up wherever others showed up, such as at the burning of three old rubber tire casings and other community events of similar magnitude.

Not that any youngster ever personally laid eyes on Uncle's gallstones, or dared to want to, or until years later even knew what gallstones were. He carried them in a Bull Durham sack, inside of which the stones were imagined to repose like diamonds from South Africa, or pearls from the Orient, treasures with strong geographical attachments, *i.e.,* stones from Gall or perhaps from Gawl.

"I took these here stones with my own knife," Uncle said, and the light of wonderment flickered in eyes around that fire. Nor was there any doubting it—"Hand over your Gawl stones" is how Uncle would have put it; and there they were, the actual stones, weighing down the dirty sack hung around his neck.

Among the other things Uncle invented was ring around the collar.

It was, as we said, some years afterward that it finally dawned on everybody what Uncle had done, which was that he performed surgery, not highway robbery, between which in those days there was a clear distinction.

Going back like this had been necessary in order to advise Professor Griner at Jonesboro that in that Bull Durham sack would have been 65 gallstones, at least. And that was 30 years before the Jonesboro lady's effort, at least.

Of Growing Old, and Grimy Joes

Mrs. R.D. Morrison of Little Rock attended a class reunion recently, 35 years after the fact, and noted that everybody had gotten older.

Except for the teachers, who had gotten younger.

Mrs. Morrison, herself, had not changed.

"A young man I had a secret crush on had lost a huge shock of dark wavy hair and it was replaced on top by something resembling a bleached bowling ball."

The bowling ball also tended toward waviness. A shock, indeed.

"He never smiled the whole time at school, but he laughed all the way through the reunion."

She had loved the first version, from a distance, but easily preferred the second.

"I can say these things because he lives in another state and does not know my married name."

She can say it, too, because of R.D. Morrison.

"My husband says the years have made a wreck of me, and no man would care what I thought, anyway."

Mrs. Morrison knows better. Most of her female classmates at the reunion had changed dress sizes several times, getting into things more comfortable as the years went by.

"But not me. My grandson looks at these old class pictures, and looks at me, and he speaks of no change at all."

Mrs. Morrison's grandson will be one year old in August.

The teachers at the reunion were ridiculous.

"Thirty-five years have passed and not one of the teachers had aged a day. I should have gone into education."

Teachers have been pulling this for years.

When we were in the first grade our teacher was 90

years old. Or maybe 114. You had to wonder how a person like that could stay awake.

Her eyesight would have shamed an eagle.

A peril faced daily in Miss Edna's class was that of being a Grimy Joe. A Grimy Joe was somebody who had dirty fingernails or who had forgotten his handkerchief.

Hence the morning showdown, fingers extended flat on the desk top, beneath them the fresh white handkerchief. Miss Edna went from desk to desk, inspecting.

A Grimy Joe got sung at. By the whole class. The escapees stood and sang, pointing at the culprit:

> *"We can beat the Grimy Joes.*
> *We step right on their toes.*
> *We make them fall and break their noses.*
> *We can beat the Grimy Joes."*

It was about more humiliation than one person could stand.

Came that fateful morning.

Grabbing and gulping, we could not find a handkerchief anywhere on our person.

The inspection had begun!

With a mighty, desperate rip, we separated the lining of our right-hand knickers pocket from the rest of the pants.

The inside of a first-grader's pocket bears no resemblance to a white handkerchief. The pocket is, in fact, an awful thing to see.

But if your teacher is bearing down, and she is 131 years old, then just maybe—

"Charles?"

Yes'm.

"What is that?"

What was what, Miss Edna?

"CHILDREN!"

They sprang and sang. Yes, how they sang. Those first-born of abominable words! What excess of cowering misery!

They sat down and we lurched up, blurting, "If it's gonna rhyme with break their noses you got to call it Grimy Joses!"

Our path to the cloakroom was swift and direct. How a woman past 150 could move like that, and with such forearm strength, that was a wonder.

Years later we saw Miss Edna.

She said, "Charles, let me see the inside of your pocket."

It was in a suit of some sort. I showed the pocket to her.

"That's better," Miss Edna said.

She wasn't half as old as she used to be. And she was beautiful.

Aw...Being One's Valentine Not Easy

At Jacksonville, Mrs. Charles Powell called her son, Jayme, inside for a behavior conference.

Jayme Powell is six. His mother sat him down.

"Did you make Lisa cry?"

Jayme said, aw, he might have.

Mrs. Powell said, "Lisa's mother said she came home bawling."

Jayme said aw.

"But, son, I thought you liked Lisa."

Jayme said, yeah, he liked Lisa.

"Then what did you do to her?" Mrs. Powell demanded.

Her son said he didn't do anything.

"She asked me to be her valentine and I said no."

That did it.

"Jayme! Why on earth don't you want to be your best friend's valentine?"

That did it for Jayme, too.

"I do!" he blurted. "But I don't know how!"

It was ever thus.

Back in the days when most of the important people were six years old, we carried those valentines around in a paper sack.

How many for a penny?

And sat under the remotest tree on the schoolground to read through those personal heartfelt expressions.

It was a mistake to think that only girls cared.

Here was a valentine shaped like a tree.

"It's for you I stand and PINE—won't you be my valentine? (signed) Marvin."

Good ole Marvin.

Here was another, a blackboard with numbered squares:

"One, two, three,

"Four, five, six,

"Seven, eight, nine—I *count* on you to be my valentine. (signed) Frederick."

Good ole Frederick. He could pick them.

Twenty-seven valentines in a paper sack.

Here was a red horse, reared high on its back feet—"I won't be horsin' around, if the valentine I've found—IS YOU! (signed) Elizabeth."

Good ole Elizabeth.

Now, here it was. The owl on the tree limb. After six trips through the paper sack, the hands begin shaking all over again.

The owl says: "Not only do I give a hoot, I give a lot of hoots to boot! Would you be my valentine? (signed) Billie Dove."

Glory be!

Would we ever have been her valentine! Right then and there!

If only we had known how.

We ache for Jayme Powell at Jacksonville that more than forty years have passed, in round, conservative figures, and still nobody has figured it out.

Oh, yes, we knew how it might have been.

And sitting beneath that schoolground tree, clutching the owl valentine, we could see it clearly: us standing before a mirror in our Humphrey Bogart undershirt, shaving with a cigarette in one corner of the mouth, on a nearby chair our Marine Corps tunic, and in the background somewhere Dick Powell singing, "Over the seas let's go, men....We're shoving right off, we're shoving right off again...It may be Shanghai...Farewell and good-bye..."—at which moment Billie Dove would walk in.

The unfeeling reader will find certain incongruities in this. A six-year-old boy shaving and smoking and shipping out with the Marines.

Somebody will say, "Why, you couldn't have even seen the mirror without standing on the commode lid. What would Billie Dove have thought about that?"

We will never know.

Because at just that moment she came around a cor-ner of the school, Billie Dove heading toward our tree, and we jumped up and ran in the other direction, fleeing to nowhere and not knowing why.

If Jayme Powell gets it figured out we would like to hear about it.

Some Birthdays Have a Certain Sting to Them

On September 16, her 63rd birthday, Gladys Chenault of Hot Springs underwent a tooth extraction, suffered a flat tire on the way home from the dentist, burned her birthday supper roast, and, in the cool of the evening, was stung by a dirt dauber.

Happy birthday, dear Gladys!

"What upset her the most was that dirt dauber."

So reports the celebrant's husband, Whit Chenault, struggling without success not to guffaw.

"I've been trying to tell her for forty years that a dirt dauber will sting like any other wasp."

Gladys Chenault made her discovery attending to some screened-in porch plants.

She still does not accept this development about the dirt dauber.

Or dobber, as the creature was generally known.

Yes, a dirt dobber won't sting, all right, in the same way a snake won't bite under water.

And in the same way an aggravated dog won't attack if you stand still and squinch your eyes.

Also, a skunk won't defoliate the environment if a potential victim waves his arms and holds his breath.

We knew a man, a kindly old gentleman, who knew all these things to be true. He went to his grave the most thoroughly stung, bitten, and sprayed individual in the history of southeast Arkansas.

It must be conceded that he never was struck by lightning in the same place twice.

The dirt dobber, in truth, does not have the hostile nature of, say, the hornet.

A hornet will look a person up and sting him just for the fun of it. There is nothing a hornet enjoys more than stinging the fire out of somebody.

The dirt dobber reacts only when put under pressure.

Step on a dirt dobber barefooted, as he is busy gathering dob, and you will wind up in a lively celebration with Gladys Chenault.

Or throw a rock at his nest.

As a youngster we threw a rock at a dirt dobber nest, having been told that the inhabitants would not sting.

Half the dirt dobbers chased us across a pasture, while the other half latched on and rode. The results were heard as far away as Arkansas City.

Yes, dirt dobbers will sting.

To make the community safe we returned to the nest. It was attached to an outbuilding of some sort, perhaps a smokehouse or perhaps not.

With a long cane fishing pole, to which gasoline-soaked rags had been tied, we set fire to the marauding dirt dobber nest.

Also we set fire to the outbuilding.

And to three acres of pasture.

Everything went to the ground. We escaped through the smoke, just ahead of five families who came running, hollering, to fight the fire. Two hours later we went back to ask what was going on.

Those dirt dobbers never bothered anybody again.

Although dirt dobbers will not sting, it is widely known what to do for the victims.

If you are ever confronted by a youngster who has been stung by a dirt dobber, quickly apply a wet baking soda paste to the sting area.

Maybe it is wet baking *powder*.

It could be instant cornbread.

Put some of that on, whatever is decided, along with a liberal pouring of turpentine.

Add a quantity of hot creosote and, facing north, crack a fresh guinea egg on the sting. This works in well with the pancake mix.

If no guinea egg is handy, then grab up the guinea itself and tear it in two. Immediately apply guinea halves to the sting area.

Three adults are needed for this. One administers the

treatments. A second subdues the victim. The third keeps reviving him so he can be aware of what is going on and get the maximum benefits.

The youngster, if he survives, will thank you for all you did.

The longest sermon in history was delivered on a July Sunday back in the late 1930s after certain McGehee youngsters were told that if they behaved in church that morning as previously, then it would follow as the night the day that all would be at least killed and probably worse.

There was to be not one squirm, one fidget, or one eye-bat, not even if the church caught fire or was swallowed up by an earthquake.

There was no fire that morning, and no earthquake.

But nine yellowjackets had taken up building something on the back of the pew ahead, just inches from the youngsters' bare knees.

When the sermon finally ended, the children had aged about ninety years.

Youngsters Well-Behaved—It's Magic

It was Friday, a busy afternoon hour at the west branch of First Jacksonville Bank.

A woman entered the lobby with two small boys, too young to be in school.

The youngsters went directly to a couch and sat down to wait.

Sibyl H. Clay, vice president and auditor of the bank, could not help admiring this behavior.

She approached the boys and offered a balloon to one.

As he took it, Mrs. Clay said, "What about your friend—would he like a balloon, too?"

The boy said, "He ain't my friend. He's my brother."

The youngster held a small stone.

"What do you have there?" Mrs. Clay asked.

"It's a magic rock," the boy said.

Mrs. Clay said, "What makes it magic?"

The boy explained, "If you hold it in your pocket, it makes you be good."

The bank officer was so impressed, she visited with the customer when her business was completed.

The customer said, "You'd be surprised how much time we spend looking for a magic rock before we go into a place. We found this one right out front here before we came into the bank."

The last time we saw a magic rock was more than forty years ago. That is a round, conservative figure.

Something went wrong with the rock, right in the middle of a haircut.

We were seated along the barbershop wall on a Saturday morning, about a dozen of us, lined up for the monthly skinning.

The victim in the chair was in agony. With face contorted, eyes squinched, shoulders hunched to protect his ears, a low and steady keening escaping his lips, along with occasional bubbles, he writhed on the humiliating board placed across the chair's arms.

Suddenly, with a violent twisting motion, he jerked one arm free from beneath the sheet, drew back, and hurled something toward the open front door.

"That sorry rock," he yelled, "it's not no damn magic!"

He was correct. The thing went right through the barbershop window.

The Dumbest Vegetable of All

With much counterfeit gagging, the sons of Mr. and Mrs. Joe Cross of El Dorado were discussing the dumbness of vegetables.

Ricky Cross, who is seven, said the dumbest vegetable of all was green beans.

Robby Cross, five, said, no, the dumbest vegetable was spinach.

His older brother insisted, "Green beans (gag) taste worse than spinach."

But Robby said, no, "They (gag) taste the same bad but spinach squirts out of your hand."

Ricky said that of all the dumb vegetables, the most undumb was mashed potatoes.

His little brother said, "That's not vegetables."

But Ricky said, "They are until you put gravy on it."

Robby said, "Yeah (gag), that's even harder to pick up than spinach."

We once got into a spinach-eating contest.

The challenger was our older brother.

You must understand the competitive nature of the relationship.

If our older brother started counting to three, to see who could jump into the old septic tank first, we jumped on the count of one.

He had the good humor, in defeat, to fall down laughing about it. We beat him so bad he decided not even to jump in.

Or take the bag swing.

"Let's race to see who gets the first swing."

Our brother, two years older, proposed this every April, as spring came to McGehee.

It was the one footrace of the year we always won.

When the swing broke and we plunged head-first into the bayou, he guessed the rope had rotted and that it was time to get a new one.

"You sure did run fast," he said, helping us out of the bayou. Although not getting too close, because we were covered with slime.

Then there was the spinach-eating contest.

"I'll bet I can eat a bowl of spinach faster than you," he said.

Personally we would rather have gone back to the septic tank.

So he heaped up two cereal bowls with cold spinach from the stove, and got out two spoons, unselfishly giving us the larger one.

"I'll time you first," he said, looking at the kitchen clock, "and then you can time me."

Noticing also the presence of hard-boiled eggs, we closed our eyes.

"Go!"

The first spoonful made our eyes water.

The second set up convulsions.

"Hurry!" our brother said, shouting encouragement.

In less than a full sweep of the kitchen clock second-hand—and because the spoon had a long handle—we got down the whole bowl of cold spinach and eggs without stopping.

Our big brother could not believe what he had seen.

In fact, he put his head down under the table and coughed and sputtered amazement and admiration.

We told him thanks.

When his head came up his own eyes were watering, but he was able to see enough to say, "Your face is green"—or something like that, because just then we sailed out the back door.

Later he came out and congratulated us again behind the chickenhouse.

"There's no use of me even trying," he admitted. "But don't tell Mom and Dad. It would sound like bragging."

It's a wonder he never got an inferiority complex.

Giving 110 Percent to "Writting"

The least useful yardstick ever devised for measuring human endeavor is the athletic expression "110 percent."

"Go out there, men, and give it 110 percent!"

To achieve this, the men must go out there and give everything it is possible to give.

And while they are out there, add ten percent to that.

Many coaches do not stop to think that probably no more than half the male population can perform in an impossible manner.

A coach once accused us, "Son, you're not giving 110 percent."

Actually we were giving 140 percent. But the result looked like 27 percent.

Driving past schoolboy football fields these late August days, you will see certain young men—set apart from the others—running laps.

The tongues of these young men are hanging out 184 percent.

They should run right off the football field, cutting across, and seek distinction in the school newspaper office.

There a person can give 200 percent just staring out the window.

This is from Stacy Malone, an eighth-grade English student who forgets to say what school:

"Our class is taking up Arkansas writting and you are the chosen subject.

"These are questions to answer.

"When is a good time to take up writting?

"Is writting fun?

"What is the best way to tell the story?

"Is satisfaction the best pay for writting?

"Other personal facts?"

To take Miss Malone's questions one at a time (a mark of good writting):

A good time for us to take up writing was when Fred Williams, a 200-pound Little Rock High School tackle, hit us on the nose with his forearm. This was in the days of no faceguards and soft helmets, when a shot to the head frequently left one looking out through his earhole.

Later a star with the Arkansas Razorbacks and the professional Chicago Bears, Fred Williams went on to weigh 260 pounds, approximately twice the weight of our new nose.

This was Raymond (Rabbit) Burnett, the high school coach, in a moment of rare compassion:

"Son, why don't you quit practice early today and take some information for me up to the school newspaper office."

"Which way is it?"

"Just follow your nose."

To take up the second question: "Is writting fun?"

Some days it is more fun than others, but every day it is more fun than getting hit in the nose.

"What is the best way to tell the story?"

The best way to tell the story is to sit down and have the power come over you. This has never happened to us, although we have been willing to sit longer than most.

We have known writers to sit down and have the power come over them, playing their typewriters for hours, like a Wurlitzer organ. At the end of the concert they are exhausted, drained of creativity, and filled with a large sense of satisfaction.

"There's really nothing like this feeling," a fellow told us once, massaging life back into his fingers. He looked very much the author. We are trying to remember something he wrote.

Charles Portis, who wrote *True Grit* and *Norwood,* told us once that he stays wary of having the power come over him.

When he begins to feel profound, Portis reaches over to a shelf near his typewriter, takes down a rain hat, and places the hat squarely on top of his head.

"Sitting there knowing how ridiculous you look, wearing a rain hat and everything, you are not as likely to try to be profound. The urge passes."

Portis writes short books, proof that the best way to tell the story is briefly.

A famous person once wrote a 22-page letter to his son who was off at college, giving the young man all the doings from home.

"I am sorry," the father said, closing out, "that I didn't have time to write you a short letter."

We always credit this quote to Benjamin Disraeli, not knowing for sure, but nobody calls our hand. It is a good thing, showing awareness, to trot out just after you have written something long and rotten.

"Is satisfaction the best pay for writting?"

Many creditors have it in their minds that satisfaction must be the only pay a person gets from writing.

Elsewhere we have undertaken another approach to answering the questions asked by Stacy Malone and her classmates. For a moment here we just felt the power come over us.

Spelling of Last Name Can Be a Taxing Problem

In downtown Little Rock, the *Arkansas Gazette* shares the neighborhood of Third and Louisiana Streets with, among others, a firm having the name Allbright in it.

Actually the firm is Albright, with one *l*. One or two *l*'s, it doesn't make much difference to persons with other names. They spell it the way it comes out. Like *banana* or *Mount Ararat*.

The United States Army wastes no time with the name at all.

As a skin-headed recruit, we inched out of ranks, green fatigues crackling, and told the sergeant about our name.

"What's wrong with it?" the sergeant roared.

We told him Allbright was supposed to have two *l*'s.

One minute he wanted mistakes reported. Now he took huge offense.

"Oh, yeah? Says who?"

The sergeant looked at the papers, reading with his finger.

"This here says only one *l*."

Holding the name down with his finger, he proposed to the entire platoon, "How many here thinks this trooper is wanting the final *l* kicked out of him?"

Forty-nine other skinheads raised a dutiful chorus, "Yes, sergeant!"

Officially, we never served in the Army.

The neighborhood firm with Albright in the name has expertise in accounting.

A letter came to us, with other mail, and we started reading before realizing the mistake.

Here was a man with income tax problems.

Ooops!

In less than a trice the letter was back inside its envelope. We saw nobody's name. The man could have been a woman. They probably were even somebody else.

The tax figures in question? We would not recognize them in a million years.

With only one letter to deliver, we traveled faster than the postman, crossing the street and taking the elevator up to the accounting firm.

In the outer office a woman sat busy with papers. There was no need to annoy her with details.

Simply, "This letter was delivered by mistake across the street."

But no need to be curt, either. We observed, turning away, that the correspondent probably would not appreciate having his tax matters show up in the Arkansas Traveler column. Just a bit of levity.

The woman paused in her work, not comprehending.

She picked up the envelope and read the name aloud, "Charles Allbright."

Something dawned on her. She put the envelope down, and looked up with a reassuring smile.

"It wouldn't have mattered if it showed up in there. He writes such a lousy column, anyway."

Heat Gives Rise to Memories of Scorchers Past

On some aluminum foil in their driveway at Fort Smith, Ronny Payne, ten, and Danny Payne, eight, put down a thermometer and got a reading of 122 degrees.

"That's hot enough to fry an egg on," Ronny said.

He went into the house, brought out an egg, and broke it on the aluminum foil.

His younger brother watched this, along with a dog named Spike, and decided he did not want an egg fried in the driveway.

"If it's hot enough to fry an egg," Danny Payne said, "it's hot enough to fry some Beenie Weenies."

He went into the house, brought out a can of Beenie Weenies, and emptied it on the aluminum foil. To this, Danny added salt and pepper and some ketchup.

His older brother watched this, along with the dog named Spike, and said, "If you'll let me have some of your Beenie Weenies, I'll let you have some of my egg."

The brothers agreed and went inside to gather eating utensils.

While they were gone the dog named Spike ate all of the Beenie Weenies and half of the egg.

Before he could finish, Mrs. Ronald Payne, mother of the cooks, returned home from the hairdresser's and drove over what was left, including the thermometer.

It is Mrs. Payne who reports on the grand experiment, concluding:

"If you think it was hot around the house before, you should have been there when their father learned it was his thirty-year-old greenhouse thermometer."

Our friend Reid was trying to remember when it had been hotter than this.

When several minutes went by and nobody else at the table said anything, Reid was able to remember.

"It was down at Camp Polk, Louisiana. Nineteen-and-fifty-four."

That was before Polk became a fort. There was nothing prissy in Reid's military experience.

"They sent our training company on a forced march. Seven miles out and seven miles back. Full field packs. That was sixty pounds. Also M-1 rifles, ten pounds, with bayonets attached, make it eleven pounds. We double-timed the whole fourteen miles with weapons at port arms."

When the company set out, the temperature stood straight up at 110 degrees.

"Of our two hundred men, a hundred-twenty were activated from the New Jersey National Guard. Half of them already wore stripes."

As he ran, Reid heard those Jersey Guardsmen going down behind him, like sacks of feed falling from a truck.

"Of course, being guidon, I could not see what was happening."

Reid was out front of everybody, having been chosen to carry the company banner. Even with that extra burden he kept pulling away in the heat, especially around the eleven-mile mark.

"But I could hear them collapsing, one after another, those poor fellows down from New Jersey, corporals and sergeants, sprawling in the gravel. Not a single one of them finished the march."

Reid never knew how many of his comrades finished. By the time the others staggered in, he had already put away the company flag, showered, got into a clean uniform, and was over at the PX starting in on his second case of 3.2 beer.

Recalling the hideous heat of that day, Reid now struck himself a blow on the forehead with the butt of his hand.

"Cancel all that! It was not 'fifty-four. That happened in nineteen-and-fifty-three."

The man is a stickler for accuracy.

From across the table, Simpson declared here was a major coincidence.

"When I first got out of the service I went to work briefly for the Highway Department Division of Statistics and Analysis."

Simpson was trying to decide whether to become a brain surgeon or go into the diplomatic corps.

On the last day of July, they sent Simpson's crew over to the West Memphis weighing station, to sit out there in the sun in Frank Buck hats and count cars and trucks going by. He was leaning toward the diplomatic corps.

"Some said it got up to 115 that day, but that was excessive."

Wild horses cannot drag an exaggeration out of Simpson.

"Actually it was only 111."

Sitting out there on the roadside, in the midafternoon heat, under that pith helmet, Simpson lost consciousness every six or seven minutes.

"One time I came to and discovered that my automatic counter had fallen from my hand. With vehicles whizzing back and forth, I grabbed for it, but the counter was sinking into the melting asphalt. I watched it go out of sight."

The rest of that afternoon, Simpson estimated cars and trucks, adding a few for each time he passed out.

"You can go over there today and see where my traffic counter sank in the pavement."

Nobody made a move to leave for West Memphis.

Our friend Reid sniffed. "What's such a big coincidence about that?"

Simpson said oh.

"In our crew was this fellow who'd been on a forced march down in Louisiana. He said he'd give anything to be back down there in a full field pack, jumping over New Jersey National Guardsmen."

Meanwhile, on a scorched practice field at Little Rock Senior High School, Coach Raymond Burnett faced 100 uniformed candidates for the Tiger varsity.

64

At his side was a smiling young assistant named Wilson Matthews.

Coach Burnett addressed the players through a shimmer of August heat waves.

"Now, girls, here is what we're going to do. We're going to run down to Camp Polk for a forced march, then we're going to run over to West Memphis and count cars, then we're going to run back here and do a few laps to warm up, and then we're going to start the practice."

Those who survived exaggerate the heat of that day. Actually it was only 112.

Traffic Counting for X-ings can be Vexing Chore

He thinks of himself, L.D. Harris does, as a person who is going through life being a responsible citizen.

His wife is no criminal, either.

Buck Harris writes from Blytheville, "As Reedie and I drive the highways and byways of this great country, we are always alert to the cautions and admonitions of road signs."

"Watch Out for Falling Rock."

"Bridge May Ice in Cold Weather." Not likely to at other times.

But for Buck Harris, it is the deer sign that is special.

"It has always intrigued me. DEER Xing. I know that a lot of deer get exed out by jumping into the paths of cars. We usually look port and starboard to see if any of these gentle creatures are ready to be exed."

The question is, how did DEER Xing get at this precise spot?

"I've wondered if highway officials put down one of those road traffic counter devices to see if the number of deer crossing deserves a sign."

And as he drives the highways and byways, looking port and starboard, Buck Harris finds other questions coming to mind.

"I've wondered about giving equal recognition to other of God's creatures crossing highways. The terrapins, the rabbits, possums, and armadillos. Even the woolly worms which are supposed to indicate the winter severity."

It happens that we have some actual experience with highway traffic counting.

Not deer traffic. Human traffic.

Fresh out of the Army, waiting to explode on the journalistic scene, we signed on temporarily with the state

Highway Department.

Division of Statistics and Analysis.

A kindly supervisor said, "Young man, do you see these forms?"

We saw them.

"Take these forms and drive to Sebastian County, where Highway 71 intersects with"—at sundown we headed west to count traffic.

At 9:00 p.m., we were sitting at a dark roadside, counting Sebastian County cars and trucks.

Also at 10:00 p.m.

It was the domino scoring system. Four short vertical lines tied together with a diagonal line—total of five.

By 10:00 p.m., we had 34 cars and 91 trucks.

It might have been the other way.

The long drive from central Arkansas to the western border left us needing sleep. Also, a large, black, image-building cigar left us nauseated.

By 10:00 p.m., we were sprawled across the seat of the Highway Department vehicle, counting roars.

If the roar sounded like a truck, we put a more or less vertical mark on the form, more or less where it said trucks.

If the roar sounded like five cars, we put four vertical marks, more or less, under cars. Then tied those together with what probably was a diagonal mark, hurling the cigar out through the window as far as we could get it without having to sit up.

In the next moment, dawn slanted through the vehicle window.

At midmorning, we handed our completed traffic count forms over to our kindly supervisor in the Little Rock office.

"Any problems, young man?"

We told him no, sir, no problems.

He pushed his hat back on his head and began studying our work, slumping and simultaneously sitting up abruptly.

67

"You show more vehicles going through than the entire 35th Division!"

We learned that later they threw our figures out on the ground of "unbelievableness."

The report speculated, "There is a strong possibility this young man went to sleep on the job."

Your Average Bachelor Does Not Understand This

Trading Pants and Places
Results in Dilemmas

In this enlightened day and time it is no longer a question of who wears the pants in the family.

Everybody wears pants.

"George, aren't those my pants you're putting on?"

"Well, I'll swear, Diane, I believe they are."

People are so equal, anything can happen.

Oh, yes, there are pockets of resistance. But resistance is being crushed under the weight of social progress. Size 44 wide.

And rightly so.

Personally, we have never been burdened with prejudice. It is our belief that any woman who is man enough to wear trousers—she, too, is entitled to first-class citizenship.

Let's see now, Julia Cordelia. These with the floweredy back pockets, they must be yours.

But that is not to say that problems won't arise.

Even in times of rampant equality.

Our man Lamar James got married.

Across the kitchen table, James and his bride, Debbie, faced each other, addressing the serious questions of combining two families.

Actually, it was a lot more serious than that.

"Actually," Lamar James says, "each of us was trying to talk the other person into becoming the family bill-payer."

James is convinced that bill-paying deserves the domestically responsible touch of a female.

"It is my belief," he says, putting it another way, "that paying bills shortens the payer's life span and threatens his sanity. Quite frankly, I was not excited about the prospect."

In other words, Lamar James would wear a tutu if it meant he didn't have to pay the bills.

So in the evening the newlyweds faced each other across the kitchen table. Each filled with compassion for the other, and with cowardice about the outcome.

Lamar James could not help noticing that his wife wore her T-shirt with the equality message on it.

Debbie's T-shirt says, "The More I Know Men, the More I Like My Dog."

Through what thoughtful procedure should a family bill-payer be chosen?

"Debbie mentioned drawing straws."

That made James uneasy.

"I suggested flipping a coin."

The newlyweds compromised by immediately throwing out each other's suggestion.

Then Debbie had another thought.

"She hit on this idea of taking our bills to my mother and letting her pay them."

But something was not right about that. What was wrong was, Lamar's mother was not about to do it.

James is not certain how the next thing happened.

Each of them, the bride and the bridegroom, produced a stack of unpaid bills, accumulated in a previous world.

The stacks sat there on the kitchen table, like the stakes of survivors in the last poker game.

Debbie carefully compared the stacks of bills.

"Yours is higher. You win!" She pushed the bills across the table.

The reporter, Lamar James, made no move to acknowledge this.

Finally, his wife struck a formula that could be agreed to. And lived with.

Debbie would count up the money owed, totaling each side. The spouse owing more money would win. That is to say, lose. That spouse would become the family bill-payer.

The bills were totaled.

Everybody is sick about the outcome.
It was a dead solid tie.

The problem in the Lamar James family remains un-
solved. Two persons cannot pay the bills, any more than
two persons can paint one picture.
Who will help?
We were going to solve it, but Julia Cordelia seems to
have made off with our trousers.

No Howling Is Allowed in This Car

HOT SPRINGS.—This is at the Holiday Inn in east Hot Springs.

A man in his mid-thirties has his car loaded, a Louisiana car, and now he is addressing four children, two boys and two girls, ranging in age from about two to about thirteen.

"Now everybody listen up before you get into the car."

Everybody listens up.

"Now before you get into the car I want it clear that there will be no pushing and shoving—right? There will be no punching each other, and no howling about who gets to sit by the window. Is everybody listening up?"

All are listening up. They are standing there in their Magic Springs caps and gorilla T-shirts, looking around in different directions, nodding, listening up.

Also listening is a woman, she too in her thirties, standing a few feet aside, both hands on a large purse, expressionless except for now and then rolling her eyes.

The father goes on, "What we are doing here is we're dealing with all this ahead of time. Do you understand? Now if everybody is ready not to do any pushing and shoving and howling and punching, we can all get in the car and go."

All get in, the woman last, and they drive slowly away.

The law was laid down on the back side of the motel. Now we are around on the front side where the Louisiana car is stopped and the man has gone into the office to settle up.

With 150 yards of the drive home to Monroe completed, the mother looks through her passenger window and says to a passerby, "Everything is okay so far."

Family travel offers a variety of pleasures.
Carsickness is only one of them.

The Louisiana family of six, with its parking lot lecture, attracted the attention of several motel guests.

One woman said of the departing mother, "She had just better hope nobody gets carsick."

Our position is to the contrary. A carsick child is a joy to travel with.

At the start of a long trip hand out Little Golden Books. "I'm getting sick," a child in the back seat will say after two miles.

Tell the child to read some more.

"I'm getting sick, too," another child will say after a few more miles.

The trick is to get them to the verge. When all are whining suitably tell them to close their Little Golden Books and their eyes.

A carsick child has no interest in punching his or her neighbor. He does not want to eat every fifteen minutes. Drive right on by Rock City. The sick child will thank you for it, if he can open his mouth.

Some Little Rock friends of ours take their children on weekend educational drives, to show them the sights of the state. They wonder why they never get any farther than Morrilton.

Well, there is no mystery about it. This family stops so often for hamburgers and french fries, by the time they get to Morrilton it is time to head back.

They carry extra ketchup in the glove compartment.

Between hamburger stops the children fight over why it's called the glove compartment.

"There's not no gloves in it!"

"Oh yeah? There might be!"

It is all very educational. What the family needs is some Little Golden Books. If the children are not going to see the sights of Arkansas, anyway, they might as well do it with their eyes closed.

Carsickness is less readily induced after dark. The landscape does not fly by in the desired manner. Children become restless and resort to gouging each other.

Tell them about the old days. Tell them how cars had no heaters, that children rode with their feet on heated bricks, which quickly cooled in the harsh cold. And no air conditioners. Bugs flew in through the windows. Tell them it took four days to go thirty miles.

No child worth his salt will listen to this. He will be snoring before he knows it.

Our readership, which is made up of people preferring a more thoughtful brand of literature, may not remember Little Golden Books.

Dad settling down in his easy chair after supper, dishes beginning to clatter softly in the sink; onto his lap squirms a tangle of knees and elbows, pajamas with feet in them, or houseshoes with roll-around animal eyes, the toes pointing outward on the wrong feet; stubby fingers clutching the literature of the evening.

Hot dog! It's time to read somebody to sleep.

"Once upon a time there was a saggy, baggy elephant...."

Then, how much later is it? From far off somewhere comes a voice, flat and indistinct, like water rising around the ears—"Paul, get off of your father and let's see if we can get him to bed."

Once we tore *The Saggy, Baggy Elephant* in half with our bare hands, no feat of strength but an accident, clutching the Little Golden Book through the rigors of a massive yawn, head back, eyes watering, suddenly to be turned loose by the yawn without warning—*RIP!*

The payoff in hush money came to something like five dollars, outrageous, but cheaper than burgling Cantrell Rexall Drug Store on a Sunday night.

Meyers Takes Lumps over "Those Tubs"

Our friend Meyers showed up in the coffeeshop with a purple lump on his forehead. The lump was covered by a Band-Aid. Or half-covered.

Meyers practically didn't know it was there.

"What lump?" he said, drinking coffee. And then, "Oh, that."

It seems that Meyers had been searching through his kitchen cabinet for a water glass. One knee slipped off the counter. He lurched sideways to recover balance, sideways and upward.

His head struck the underside of the cabinet door.

It was nothing.

A bachelor at our table spewed coffee over most of the group. He had trouble settling down.

"Knees?" the bachelor said finally. "What were you doing up there on your knees?"

Meyers was not amused.

"I told you—I was looking for a drinking glass."

Meyers's wife is good about saving plastic food containers. Empty oleo "tubs" are her favorites. Those and frozen whipped cream cartons. And especially Mrs. Somebody's pimiento cheese holders.

"The pimiento cheese are clear," Meyers pointed out. "If you ever decide to put anything in the container, you can look in there and see what you put in."

Meyers's wife has stored away scores of those empty containers in their kitchen cabinet. Hundreds, actually. Most have their original lids.

Six months ago Meyers asked where the drinking glasses were.

"They're out in the garage," Mrs. Meyers said. "We need more cabinet space."

Your average bachelor does not understand this. He thinks selfishly about getting a drink of water.

Nor does every married man comprehend.

We know a fellow who got into it with his wife over chicken pot pie pans.

His wife stored up, oh, 300 chicken pot pie pans. And maybe 200 beef pot pie pans. That small crinkly kind, just right for saving. And cherishing.

She threw them out after they fell out of the cabinet on her husband.

It wasn't the pain. Pot pie pans don't hurt that much, even when they're falling in towers.

But the pans just kept falling, raining down on her husband's head, until he lost control.

"What in blazes do you want with all these fool pans?"

Her lower lip quivered. She knelt and started picking up pans.

He got down there, too—"I mean, just explain it to me, why do we want to keep all these pie pans?"

Her lip quivered. "I don't know. I just thought, well, maybe someday they might come in handy. We might get a cat or something that needs feeding."

A cat? Yes, but 500 cats!

She took her little pot pie pans out and threw them in the trash.

Her husband felt rotten the rest of the day.

He shouldn't have. In the middle of the night she went out to the trash and got all her pie pans back, kicking away assorted cats.

We have a friend whose wife saves concentrated orange juice containers.

"She cuts both ends out and saves the empties in drawers."

His wife says orange juice containers make excellent biscuit cutters.

"We now have 77 biscuit cutters. Or 154 if you count cutting biscuits with both ends."

Personally we would never manage to hang on to all this quirky junk. Not and keep room enough for our jelly jars.

No Need to Worry, You Can Always Use "Whatever"

Our friend Reid has given up extensive use of the word "whatever."

Reid stood in the carport, facing his storage room door, and declared to Mrs. Reid, "I'm going to spend all weekend straightening this place up."

Mrs. Reid thought that was an excellent idea.

"What are you going to do first?"

Reid stared into the storage room and said, "Whatever."

He went back into the house.

That was the first week in April. So far as Mrs. Reid knows, her husband has not thought about the storage room since then.

Reid is moving along toward maturity. Some might say he has moved a little beyond it.

We ran into Reid at the grocery store. He was puzzling over a shopping list.

"What do you suppose she wants with two pounds of potato chips? That's a tremendous amount of potato chips."

The list did not say potato chips. It said "P. Cps." We pointed out to Reid that "P. Cps." meant pork chops.

He looked again at his list and said, "Well, whatever."

We saw Reid pushing his cart out of the grocery store. Somehow he had decided that "P. Cps." meant plastic cups. Cups were falling out everywhere.

The two pounds of plastic cups are in his storage room.

Mrs. Reid is trying not to worry.

Fortunately there is nothing to worry about. When Mrs. Reid's husband throws in the word "whatever" he is talking fashionable language.

Johnny Carson asks a guest attired in a short skirt,

"Otherwise, what are your interests?"

The guest rearranges herself and says, "Oh, the zither, cardiovascular poems...whatever."

It saves a lot of time.

Throughout history the use of "whatever" could have saved centuries of time.

"To be or not to be...whatever."

"Four score and...whatever."

"Do you, Phil, take this woman to have and to...whatever."

It's too bad nobody had thought up "whatever" when Jimmy Oates got up on the stage in Pottsville to play his recital piece, "In a Little Wigwam."

After months of rehearsal, the young pianist sat down and stared at the keyboard, suddenly not knowing tee from pee.

After several minutes he stood up and walked off the stage, mouth white and ears aflame.

Nowadays that same pianist can get up from the bench, face the audience and say "whatever," then make a fashionable exit.

Reid's wife is not comforted by the modern language.

"Frankly," she confides, "when my husband stops and says 'whatever' I think he's lost track of what he was talking about. I'm afraid his mind is beginning to go."

She feared this most recently Sunday.

"My husband has been elected president of our Sunday school class."

Reid's duties as class leader are not terribly challenging.

"First, he appoints somebody to take up the collection. Next he gives the announcements. At the end he dismisses the class."

Last Sunday Reid forgot to appoint a collection taker.

He got up and gave an announcement: "The preacher told me to emphasize that attendance next week will be very important because we're going to discuss...whatever."

He dismissed the class—"See everybody next...when-ever."

Mrs. Reid doesn't see how it could be worse.

It could be. She could have two pounds of pork chops out there in her storage room.

Wintertime Brings on Attacks of Hogrophobia

It is time to denounce gluttony.

Across Arkansas, distraught persons are holding their sides. And their heads.

Distraught and disbelieving persons.

"I could not have eaten all that!" our friend Reid confronted his wife accusingly.

"You ate more!" declared Mrs. Reid, a sweet potato stored in each jaw.

Reid had kept his pre-Christmas fitness vow.

"Wherever I go, I shall walk!"

For a week he walked. From the fruitcake to the eggnog. Over to the fudge. Back to the pecan pie.

Mrs. Reid, two years younger and a health freak, ran between and among these destinations.

To rid themselves repeatedly of the sweet taste, the Reids grazed through four acres of breakfast cereal chex. Heavily buttered and salted.

Late Sunday, Reid demanded an end to it.

"I am appalled," he said to Mrs. Reid, "that you could allow this to happen."

The word "appalled" released a huge puff of powdered sugar from Reid's upper lip.

At what must have been her day's bleakest moment, Mrs. Phillips telephoned from west Little Rock. Her voice was shrill and projecting.

"Can you hear me? There is so much ice on the line!"

Mrs. Phillips first called last April. At the height of a tornado alert.

"You will have to speak louder," Mrs. Phillips shouted back in April. "I am wearing a crash helmet."

She was telephoning from her bathtub. Mrs. Phillips and her neighbor, elderly Mr. Maxwell, were riding out the tornado in the tub, taking turns wearing the crash helmet for 30-second intervals.

Even during the worst of that tornado scare, with the siren wailing, and Mrs. Phillips crouched there in the tub shouting through her helmet—that was nothing compared with the anxiety in her voice this week.

"I'm here alone, and I have to have some help!" Mrs. Phillips said. She added something that sounded like, "Smurmf, chomp, smack."

Mrs. Phillips was eating a head of cabbage.

Not for four days has Mrs. Phillips been out of her house.

Snow and ice trapped her, front door and back.

"I have been eating twenty-four hours a day. The rest of the time I think about food."

Mrs. Phillips began eating back on—what day was it?—with a small helping of pinto beans.

"You can do only so much to the inside of a house."

She did the inside of the house and then stood at her living room window, looking out, arms folded.

Tight-lipped.

During snowstorms, Mrs. Phillips suffers from hogrophobia—a fear of eating oneself out of house and home.

The sickness is self-fulfilling.

"I am calling," Mrs. Phillips said, "because I have started hearing the carts."

She explained the carts.

"When you're in the hospital, recovering from surgery, just lying there, nothing to do except look at your watch, you start listening for the carts out in the hallway, the carts bringing the next meal."

Snowbound at home, she was hearing the carts.

What you do, Mrs. Phillips said, veering off without explanation, is put the cornbread in the bottom of the bowl.

"Put the cornbread, crumbled up, in the bowl, and on top of that you put a large helping of slaw. Then you ladle in two big ladles of pinto beans, with plenty of hot juice to soak the cornbread."

Of course, you will want Tabasco sauce.

"When you eat all of that," Mrs. Phillips said, "you eat another bowl just like it. Then another bowl. And another."

Back when she lived in Iowa, land of many snowfalls, Mrs. Phillips's husband took to calling her "Hamp."

"I don't know what he meant, something affectionate."

Mrs. Phillips's husband was a swine farmer, raising mostly Hampshires.

One day he drove away in the snow, leaving no forwarding address.

So for four days Mrs. Phillips had been pinned down in western Little Rock—or penned up—and now she was out of pinto beans and cornmeal, and she was grazing on her last cabbage, a head previously owned by elderly Mr. Maxwell, who had rolled it across the ice to her door, like a farmer pitching hay from a truck.

Just prior to that, Mrs. Phillips had jumped up, propelled by another attack of hogrophobia, and made six pounds of pecan fudge—"Something to get rid of that pinto taste."

In a moment of high courage, she threw the fudge out—all but five pounds of it.

Which sharply reminded her of something.

"I have go to now. The carts are coming!"

The Age of Embarrassment

At Fort Smith, Herschel Pogue got into one of those embarrassing situations in which a person does not know his own age. Men acquiring a little maturity come by this honestly.

Pogue was sitting in a bank, filling out a form, which is not one of life's more relaxing procedures in the first place.

Across the desk a young lady assisted with a melodic voice and a pretty red fingernail—your name here, your place of employment—"Your age goes on this little spot."

Pogue tells how it was:

"My mind raced. I thought I was going to be fifty-four, or maybe I already had been. Things just suddenly went blank."

The matter wasn't resolved until Pogue got out his driver's license, reddening, to consult the date of his birth. The young lady did the arithmetic.

"Sir, that makes you fifty-six."

"Yes," Pogue said. He hurried to explain his confusion, "But you'll notice that's a new driver's license. It doesn't go into effect until next month."

A week later, Pogue still does not understand why he said that; no more than he understood, subsequently, why the bank accepted his business.

More than likely it was the red fingernail.

The older a man gets, the more confused he can get about his age. It is not his fault.

We know a fellow who during the great snowfall and glazeover was persuaded to believe he practically was ready for the Superstars competition.

"A man no older than you," his wife said, "you should be able to go out there and clear the driveway without working up a sweat." She pushed him out the door with a shovel.

About the sweating, she was right. It was 22 degrees

out there.

"But with that kind of buildup, I felt a fresh surge of strength."

So what happened?

"I think I might have hurt my back. After about an hour I was standing out there, taking a little break in the action, watching this young lady across the street scraping ice from her windshield in a form-fitting snowsuit."

The man's wife opened the door and hollered at him, louder than was necessary.

"Come inside, you old fool, before you have a heart attack."

For one who aged so much in an hour, he was philosophical about it. Even the Superstars get to choose only seven of the ten events.

A friend of ours got a running suit and shoes for Christmas. Actually, the clothes are not all that fast. A wobbling trot is about their top speed. But the new gear made our friend feel young, walking around the neighborhood.

Until last week.

"Hey! My ball rolled down in the sewer." It was a neighborhood youngster, about eight.

"Oh?" our friend asked.

"My mother won't let me get down in the sewer," the youngster said. He added, admiringly, "I'll bet you could get down there and get it easy."

Our friend begged off. "Son, if I got down there I'd probably never get out."

The lad's expression changed.

"How old are you?"

Our friend said he was in his forties.

"Is that all the old you are?" the youngster said. "I guess with that suit on you're a scuba diver for Roto-Rooter."

We have been fortunate never to have had the age problem. When we were only sixteen, a wise mother snapped this unforgettable wisdom at us:

85

"Son, you're old enough to know you're too young to do that!"

Without that sort of guidance, a sixteen-year-old could set out in life penalized—not having the head start of knowing he was behind.

It gave us the good sense never to set out at all.

Would They Come and Find Him Slightly Ajar?

Old Avery Was Whistling in the Dark

Rain was starting to fall on the parking lot at Baptist Medical Center when we ran into our old classmate Avery.

Acres of cars were jammed in there. Avery was walking among the cars in what was marked Section B. He was changing directions frequently and appearing nonchalant.

We asked Avery what was up.

"Fine," he said.

It was not a very sensible answer.

Avery looked around among the cars, eyes darting here and there. He was whistling and humming at the same time.

"I am out for a walk," he explained, rain water dangling from his nose. "I really enjoy getting out on a day like this."

Obviously the man had lost his car. Even a fool could see as much. He had no more idea than a betsy-bug where he had parked before going into the hospital.

It is amazing how many persons get into this fix. Stand out there and watch them. If it's raining, put a newspaper over your head. They are walking this way and that, stopping, muttering, looking for their cars. Some run in a variety of directions.

We said goodbye to Avery, pretending no awareness of his difficulty.

The next time we saw Avery was 20 minutes later. The rain was falling harder and he had made it over to—it must have been Section G. This was 400 yards from our first meeting. Four hundred yards and maybe 10,000 cars, most of them, if not all, looking the same.

We said it was nice seeing him again, and asked how his family was.

"You bet," Avery said, looking here and there.

His shoulders were up around his ears, and much of

the rain was going down his shirt collar. He must have been having the time of his life.

In truth, the man looked like an absolute dunce, standing there in the downpour. But we stood there with him, under our newspaper, never letting on.

A vehicle crawled toward us, the hospital security van with wipers whomping.

Avery resumed whistling. Then suddenly he remembered something.

"There is one other person I forgot to visit," he said. "My mother had her gall bladder removed this morning." He took off walking stiffly in the direction of the Medical Center.

Vanity reduces men to curious behavior. Was Avery afraid of being thought of as senile? Or as a common parking lot thief? It is unbecoming in a classmate.

For our part, we quickly opened the nearest car door and rearranged things in the back seat until the security van inched past.

It was down in parking Section A, 500 yards away, that we ran into Avery a half-hour later.

His visit had been cut short, he said, because his mother checked out of the hospital and went home.

This had gone on long enough.

We volunteered our memory plan to Avery, a sure-fire procedure for keeping track of a parked car.

"Why would I want to know a thing like that?" he objected, whistling. The whistles did not come easily any more. His lips were shriveling and beginning to change color.

The memory procedure was simply this:

When you park at a place such as Baptist Medical Center, where there are maybe 20,000 cars, pay careful attention to where you are. If it is Section C, then make up a rhyme—say, "C is for *me.*" If it is Section F, then say, "F is for *find.* I'll *find* my car in F."

"That doesn't rhyme," Avery whistled.

Yes, and F also stands for fool. Any man who will argue while he's drowning does not deserve to be helped.

It was the last we saw of Avery.

Another sure-fire way is to check into the hospital. Get yourself a room and stay there until about midnight. The lot clears out by then and you can more or less find your car.

Gourmet Sports Fan Plans To Get Rich Quick

Somebody has been generous enough to include us in a crackerjack business venture through which, in four weeks, we will make $108,000 selling our own recipes.

In four weeks!

That's more money than we've made selling our recipes in four years.

But this whopping new income virtually is assured:

"Friends, this is *not* a chain letter. IT IS A PERFECTLY LEGAL MULTILEVEL MARKETING PLAN!!!"

All we do is send two dollars each to four persons whose names are listed at the bottom of the offer. "That's eight dollars for four good recipes, the same as you would pay through the *Enquirer* or *Globe* for a recipe."

Then right off, by return mail, we will learn to prepare "Tangy Rhubarb Crisp" (the recipe of a man in Minnesota), "M&M Cookie Delight" (another man in Minnesota), "Grow Large Vegetables" (a man in Alabama), and "Corn Fritters" from our own benefactor in Arkansas.

But forget the recipes.

By removing the top name on the list and adding our own at the bottom, we are on our way to making a nifty $108,000.

The plan instructs:

"Make 100 copies of this letter and distribute it to friends, relatives, neighbors, even strangers at the supermarket, who might have recipes to sell. That's all there is to it!"

The results will make our postman curse.

Based on merely a fifteen percent response, by the end of a month we will receive 54,240 letters from persons mailing in two dollars each.

That's $108,480.

The last time we heard of such a crackerjack deal, some fellow ran a classified ad in a southern California newspaper.

91

He listed a post office box and said, "This is absolutely the last day to send in your two dollars."

Some responders rushed in four dollars, making doubly certain not to be left out.

The man received thousands of dollars and, if we remember correctly, three years in prison.

Our plan is to slip the postman some recipes on the side.

Having just completed a big football weekend in front of the television set, we are splendidly prepared to enter into this lucrative venture.

Our recipe is in fact four recipes, wrapped up as a Game Watcher's Special. It should rank up there with "Tangy Rhubarb Crisp."

Tropical Tantalizer:

Take a banana. Peel it. Eat the banana.

During a commercial get up and throw the peeling into the kitchen wastebasket.

Tyrolean Yodel Wurst:

Open a can of Vienna sausages. Hold the can under the sink faucet and wash that stuff off, averting your gaze. Diners who object to torn-up Vienna sausages should open both ends of the can and push the Yodel Wursts through.

Eat in front of the television set with half a box of crackers.

Seafood Surprise:

Ideal for postgame victory diners.

Open a can of sardines, preferably costing more than a quarter.

Eat in front of the television set, watching replays, with the other half of a box of crackers.

The surprise is how much Tabasco sauce you spilled into the seafood can.

Keep cat kicked away with feet.

Autumn Harvest Glacé:

Satisfying windup for a gourmet day.

With television set turned off, stand in silence of kitchen and eat a bowl of Sugar Frosted Flakes. Read cereal box, ignoring sounds of teeth crunching on plastic. Slow readers might need to eat two bowls.

Webb Held Hostage by Neighbor's Devotion

Our friend Webb, coming down with his annual spring cold, confided that his neighbor, Miss Edwina, was a good woman in the worst sense of the word.

"Miss Edwina will do anything for you," Webb said, "except spare you."

He went into a sneezing fit.

"I am not going to get this cold. My overall health simply is not up to it."

Webb was as grateful as the next person. He appreciated everything done for him.

But the last time he got down with a cold, his neighbor, Miss Edwina, came knocking on the door at 6:45 in the morning.

"She brought my newspaper to me."

Webb was stumbling back into bed when the door was knocked on again.

"She had a gallon of hot grapefruit juice."

Webb protested—"At least let me pay for it."

Miss Edwina heard none of that. "My work is my reward," she told him.

Webb was returning again to bed when Miss Edwina appeared a third time, bearing a folder about allergies and a volume of golden verse.

"She read golden verses to me all morning, and kept pouring that hot grapefruit juice." Webb went pale, telling about it.

At noon, Miss Edwina apologized for leaving briefly to feed somebody's bird. She was back before Webb could down a round of aspirin.

"All afternoon she kept my spirits up, detailing her activities in the Association of Retired Persons."

Or maybe that was not the organization.

"Maybe it was the Associate Reformed Presbyterians." At midafternoon he had plunged into a coma of some sort.

"Their initials are very similar," Webb pointed out.

He was certain that both were wonderful organizations.

"I look forward to joining them someday. It's just that right now..."—our friend was peering out through a venetian blind.

While her husband lived, Miss Edwina kept them on the go in interesting activities. He was a quiet, kindly man. Neighbors thought of him as "Mr. Edwina."

One day after forty years, for no apparent medical reason and offering no discernible resistance, Mr. Edwina took to his bed and went his way.

Since that time Miss Edwina had been free to devote all her time and energies to the care of others.

"Right now," Webb declared, his head between the blind slats, "I am going cambig."

Cambig?

"Out in the woods. I have a pup tent. I'll go camb in the woods. There must be a dry spot out there subwhere."

He was startled by movement in the front yard. It was only a man reading the meter.

"She comes over this time every day to make sure there is nothing valuable in my mailbox. That's on her way to telling the Johnsons that their dog is out again. And to getting a better look at the strange car parked in front of the Hudspeths."

Webb said that few persons were fortunate enough to have a neighbor like Miss Edwina. But those who did knew full well how fortunate they were.

In a dream, Webb saw Miss Edwina as the head parole officer.

"I know that doesn't make sense," he said, "but it might produce some remarkable results in criminal reform."

In his dream, Webb saw two men sentenced to six visits from Miss Edwina.

"You understand, I am telling this only in the most respectful way."

Webb related the events of his dream.

"One man went absolutely straight. He was never heard from in criminal circles again."

The other?

"After two visits he turned himself back in at the prison, saying he had no right to be on the outside."

We last saw Webb peering through the slats, planning to take his idea to the authorities when he got back from the woods. If he could make it to the car.

Lunch Thief Puts Damper on Annual Parade

At Bisbee, Arizona, last week a man was sentenced to five years in prison for stealing a ham and cheese sandwich.

Five years seems stiff for a ham and cheese.

But this fellow did not have a sparkling record. Now he will have an opportunity to think things over.

We must report a sandwich thief at Little Rock.

A baloney bandit.

On the morning of the State Fair parade an alleged man entered the Arkansas Gazette Building and left in a hurry with two sandwiches.

The sandwiches were in a paper bag, brown in color.

The thief was chased from the building by representatives of Pickens-Bond Construction Company, our upstairs neighbor, from which he also stole an alleged soft drink to go with the baloney sandwiches.

We report this as a civic duty.

Those were our alleged sandwiches.

A word of background would help.

Over the years on State Fair parade day a colleague, Mrs. Pat Best, has left her station to come to our window and watch the parade down below.

We have known Mrs. Best for years, her husband for longer than that. So she has felt no constraint in coming to our window in the name of old friendship.

Not hogging the window, exactly. But nobody is getting any littler these days.

Mrs. Best always brought her lunch to the window. She was thoughtful enough, between bites, to point out such things as "Here comes the band from Smackover" or "Look at those neat costumes."

This helped us immeasurably in figuring out what was going on.

Mrs. Best never had any lunch left over.

A year ago as the sweeper pushed the last of the alleged parade down the street, Mrs. Best finished off a cake snowball of some sort and bade her customary farewell, "Same time next year?"

Not that we were upset. But that coconut on her mouth was the flake that broke the camel's back.

She professed chagrin—"Why, of course! I should have thought of it. Next year I'll bring you a lunch, too."

Last week before the parade we met Mrs. Best in the hall and reminded her of the new arrangement.

Later we reminded her again, to spare possible embarrassment.

The day before the parade we reminded her that two sandwiches might be better than one.

Then came parade day.

At midmorning Mrs. Best appeared at our desk red-faced.

"Did you take your lunch from my stockroom?"

We informed her that a person whose job is thinking large thoughts hardly goes around poking early into lunch sacks.

She disappeared in a state of agitation.

Minutes later Mrs. Best was back—"He stole your lunch! He stole your lunch!"

This was her animated account:

Hearing reports of a possible lunch thief in the building, Mrs. Best went upstairs to Pickens-Bond and, yes, they had pursued a man running with a paper sack and one of their own soft drinks.

On the side of the sack—get this—on the side of the lunch sack, the alleged Pickens-Bond spokesman said, was written "Charlie."

A more elaborate piece of fiction had not come along since *Gone with the Wind.*

What kind of fool did Mrs. Best take us to be?

But she was inconsolable—detailing the inventory of the lunch sack down to the last item: two baloney sandwiches, dill pickles, chips, and Twinkies. Yes, and a banana!

To go along with the charade, we agreed to eat Mrs. Best's lunch during the parade. Not all of it. We saved her a small bite of pickle and one chip.

It is somewhat disturbing to remember that as we threw away the empty sack, we saw written on the side of it, "Mine."

Why would a woman who brought only one sack to work do that?

Three Revelations on a Sunday Morning

For his sermon topic last Sunday Rev. John Turner of Pulaski Heights Christian Church chose the joy of discovering God's power.

Which is not to say that there is joy in all of man's discoveries.

For example, when John Turner arrived at the church Sunday morning he discovered that he had left his sermon at home.

There was still plenty of time.

Mr. Turner made the return drive home, about two miles. He found his sermon on the breakfast table and there made a second discovery.

The message was soaking wet. John and Judy Turner's eighteen-month-old daughter, Carissa, earlier had done her breakfast number there.

"I remembered seeing her playing at the table. She had turned a glass of water over on my sermon."

By shaking and wiping, the minister managed to save his words for the morning.

"They were somewhat blurred," he recalled.

But Mr. Turner left the house in good shape for the work ahead.

Which was when he made his third discovery of the morning.

"I guess it was just as I closed the door, locked it, that I realized I'd left the keys inside."

Car key and door key.

The joy of discovering how to get into a locked house when it's time to be getting to church is not joy unrestrained.

The minister, in fact, could *not* get back into his house.

Except for one long-shot possibility.

The Turners have a dog, Rowsby Woof. Down at the bottom of the back door Rowsby Woof has her own door, hinged access to the back yard, and a way back inside.

The minister of Pulaski Heights Christian Church went around back, got down on his knees, and surveyed the situation. It was not promising.

As the church secretary, Sheila Bowman, would put it later, "No, his size would not help him get through a dog's door."

Mr. Turner took off his coat.

Then he took off his vest.

He got down and began to squirm into Rowsby Woof's door.

At this point it depends on which member of the congregation you are talking to.

Some say their minister backed through the dog's door feet first.

Others say, no, it was the other way. Still others say the preacher employed several versions of both, more or less coming and going at the same time—it is difficult to get the accounts straight because all the tellers are laughing their heads off, in a respectful manner of course.

The minister's personal accounting to us suggests a conventional head-first entry—"Rowsby was licking my face practically the whole time."

That was more Sunday morning fun than Rowsby had come to expect.

Now John Turner made his largest discovery of the morning.

"I was stuck in the door. I just got to a place where I couldn't go any farther and I couldn't back out, either."

Never mind the success of the project.

"I accomplished what I set out to do. Once I got far enough inside I was able to reach up and open the door. But that didn't help me."

When a man is *part* of a door it doesn't much matter whether he is opened or closed.

Mr. Turner struggled, and he longed for the power of discovery.

Did he hear angel voices?

"I began to have images. What would be happening at

101

the church?"

Would they come and find him slightly ajar?

Something inspired John Turner to free himself. How long it took he cannot say. Probably not the eternity that went by.

"I just worked at it until I got out. Maybe I wasn't stuck much more than five minutes."

He hurried to the church with his blurred sermon, arriving with just a minute to spare.

Unfortunately, during that minute he explained to somebody what had happened. The account was passed on to somebody else, and then to still a third member of the congregation.

When pulpit time came there was nothing to do but get up there and tell the whole thing.

Breakfasts of Friskies and Meow Mix

Some Guests Just Take Too Many Liberties

For years a raccoon family has been coming to Gladys Hamilton's home in Pulaski Heights.

Not only the immediate raccoon family, but friends of the family, too. Other raccoons.

They come for meals, an innumerable caravan, in the early morning. Breakfasts of Friskies and Meow Mix.

Gladys Hamilton's son, W.J. Hamilton, describes the feeding procedure.

"The food is left on a table on the porch so that the creatures can be observed as they come to feed at four every morning."

Mrs. Hamilton has treasured the visits.

"You should see their little paws when they pick up their food and eat. They are just so sweet."

In the creatures' eyes she can see gratitude.

A raccoon without his Friskies is not a grateful raccoon.

Do not ask Gladys Hamilton how, after all these years, she forgot to put the food out.

She will not forget again.

Having fallen asleep on the sofa, Mrs. Hamilton was awakened in the dead of morning by unearthly noises.

This good woman is not given to excessive language.

"I was lying there on the sofa and all hell was breaking loose all around me."

Don't ask Bill Hamilton how his mother forgot to put out the raccoon breakfast.

When their Friskies and Meow Mix weren't on the porch table, the creatures got together.

"Hungry and determined to get their usual meal, they marched to the side of the house."

Around there is a swinging door, a two-way arrangement that enables family pets to come and go.

"The raccoon family, along with its friends, marched to the side of the house and came in through the doggie door."

What is the sound of all hell breaking loose?

Bill Hamilton relates, "Cautiously the creatures advanced into the living room where they were greeted by a snapping, yipping chihuahua which fears no animal on earth, and by a jumping and barking Pomeranian."

That was just the animal racket.

"All this plus the screams of my mother and her broom flailing the air threw the raccoons into a frenzy. In their efforts to escape they climbed up walls and under furniture."

Gladys Hamilton was sorely challenged.

"I knew that if I opened the front door I could run the raccoons out. But one of the dogs would have run out, too. And if she ever got out she would just keep going."

Daylight revealed a disaster area.

Bill Hamilton got to his mom's house about twelve hours after the creatures came in demanding breakfast.

"When I arrived on the scene everything in the room that was breakable had been, with the exception of one mirror." Vases, lamps—"I thought I'd be able to repair some of the glassware, but none was salvageable."

At 10:00 a.m., when she thought she was alone again, Mrs. Hamilton found a raccoon still hiding behind a door.

Bill Hamilton: "At 4:00 p.m. two more raccoons were discovered wedged between the upper sash and outer window cover in a bedroom."

It turned out that almost nobody had left the house.

The raccoons in the bedroom were no trouble. All Hamilton had to do was remove the windowframe. It took only an hour.

An Amazing Feat by Rex, the Wonder Dog

This is the remarkable story of Rex, a faithful dog who beat his master home from the hunt.

Across a distance of eighteen miles.

Through alien woodlands.

In rain and darkness.

At last along busy city streets.

If Vernon Bayliss lives to be 100—those are his words to persons hearing the remarkable story—if Bayliss should make 100 he would never figure out how Rex did it.

The tale is fraught with anxiety and heartache.

And ultimate exultation!

Rose Bayliss, wife of the faithful dog's master, has been generous enough to share it.

The Baylisses live in southwest Little Rock.

Near dusk on Friday Vernon Bayliss left home bound for a hunting camp in Perry County.

He said goodbye to Rose and instructed his dog, Rex, to get into the back of the pickup truck.

Rex was not enthusiastic. He is a two-house dog, one in the back yard and another in the pickup truck.

But outside the carport shelter rain was falling.

Faithful Rex had to be more or less stuffed into his traveling quarters.

Thus did the hunter depart for the hill.

Reaching a store near Shinall Mountain, Bayliss stopped for some hunting essentials. Chewing tobacco. A case of light beverage. Several pounds of potato chips.

For Rex he bought two packages of bacon-flavored jerky, the dog's favorite.

Through the rain, Vernon Bayliss carried his supplies back to the truck. It was good to be on the hunt.

Rex was not in his traveling quarters. Having stowed the hunting supplies up front, Bayliss opened a package of jerky and offered it through the door of the doghouse. But Rex was not in there.

The hunter looked around to see where his dog might be stretching his legs.

"Rex?"

The call produced nothing.

"REX!"

Bayliss got into the truck and started the engine, a sign for his dog to get a move on.

Just then another truck pulled up, nullifying the effect. The occupants of the second truck went into the store for hunting supplies.

For fifteen minutes Bayliss walked the area, calling his dog.

Then he left the store light, moving in darkness back along the highway, calling.

Twice his eyes played harsh tricks on him, perceiving nonexistent forms on the rain-slicked highway. Twice the hunter's heart skipped a beat.

Against that heart's judgment—"Don't move the truck"—Bayliss returned to his vehicle and began driving, up and down the highway, on side roads, slow and then fast, looking, stopping to call his dog's name. Listening to silence.

It is only now, hearing the man tell it, that the anxiety can be endured, so bright now is the light in his eyes and so deep the pride in his voice.

As Rose Bayliss heard her husband detail it that first of many times on the telephone:

"It was after midnight when I got back home—there wasn't any way I could go on to camp.

"I drove ten miles in every direction and stopped at every store and every house—even got this one old couple out of bed. I told everybody in the county Rex's name and where I lived, and they could name their reward."

Then the fantastic ending.

"When I turned into the driveway there he was! Back home! Brother, that's almost eighteen miles in six hours! And at night!"

He has heard of some amazing animal feats. But if Vernon Bayliss lived to be 100, well, Rex just blew them all away.

So Rose Bayliss had to make her decision.

"I don't care how many of his buddies he brags to, but this morning he said he was going to send it off to True Dog Stories, whatever that is."

What her husband doesn't know, according to the woman who watched from the carport door, was that faithful Rex, the wonder dog, jumped out of that pickup truck before it got halfway out into the rain.

He never left home.

Fabulous Foster Rivals Rex, the Wonder Dog

Thanks to leadership provided by remarkable Rex, the wonder dog, we can now disclose the equally breathtaking feat of fabulous Foster.

Foster is a dog owned by Paul and Louise Simmons of Hot Springs.

Some say the dog owns the people.

But to review.

Rex, the wonder dog, beat his master home from a hunting trip.

As Vernon Bayliss of Little Rock marveled to countless friends on the telephone:

"He got back before I did...nearly eighteen miles...pitch dark in a rainstorm...and at the end old Rex had to go the whole length of University Avenue through all that traffic, unless he went around town on the interstate. If I live to be 100 I'll never figure out how he did it."

Rose Bayliss had to put a stop somewhere. Her husband was about to pack up and take his dog to "Those Amazing Animals."

How remarkable Rex did it was by never leaving home in the first place. He hopped out of the pickup truck just as his master pulled out of the carport into the rain.

Vernon Bayliss has made no more telephone calls. He is getting quite a few.

As remarkable as that was, listen to the feat of fabulous Foster.

Also listen to the feet. Foster weights 80 pounds.

The distance from the picnic spot, where they first missed Foster, back to the Simmons home was exactly 31 miles. Twisting, turning, traffic-clogged miles, the open road with turnoffs, and three bridges to cross.

At the picnic site, Paul Simmons had opened the back door of his recreational vehicle and turned away, not even looking in, allowing Foster time to arouse himself from his traveling nap.

That afternoon turned into an emotional nightmare.

After dark the Simmonses pulled into their driveway, exhausted, heartsick, planning Lost and Found ads, then to round up supplies and return to the picnic ground at daybreak.

But there!

In the headlights in the driveway!

"FOSTER!"

What a feat that was!

In fact, what feet those were, now splayed across the driver's side window. And Foster's face between them.

All that searching, the calling out, the increasing heaviness of hearts, the pain of swallowing—the Simmonses don't mind saying it, sitting there in the driveway, being looked at by that face, through those paws, they dissolved in tears.

Then out of the cab to maul and be mauled, to roll and tumble and shout, such excess of joy.

Thirty-one miles!

"It will never happen again," Paul Simmons said later to the amazing dog. "The next time Mama puts you in the van she'll ride back there with you. One of us will."

"Me?" Louise Simmons said. "I didn't put him in the van!"

"You didn't? You *had* to! Because I sure didn't!"

What fabulous Foster thought, reclining by the hearth, is not recorded.

He looked up periodically, though, with an expression that said, "I don't know where you were all day, but let's go back out in the yard and do that again."

No More Dog Stories from "Crazy Fools," Please

A man who identified himself as "Mr. Sloan" appeared at the office door demanding no more dog stories.

"I am fed up with it," he said, making fed-up gestures. "I'm tired of seeing human feelings ascribed to dogs."

Mr. Sloan said people were "crazy fools" about dogs.

"I have a dog. Do you think she gives two hoots in hell what I'm thinking?"

We have not met Mr. Sloan's dog. Probably she could be forgiven a bit of indifference.

But he knew the answer.

"No, she doesn't give two hoots. She doesn't give one hoot!"

We asked whether Mr. Sloan had considered trading his dog in for an owl.

But he was in no mood for solutions.

Of course, Mr. Sloan is correct.

When it comes to their dogs, people are bigger fools than anybody else.

It is a comfort to find a dog owner with a level head.

"Teasha has been with us the past year and a half," explains a level-headed Little Rock woman. "We treat her like what she is—a stray dog. This is especially true when she goes bye-bye in the car-car."

Identified as a peke-a-poo, Teasha showed up at the estimated age of thirteen.

"She arrived with glazed-over cataract eyes, a few teeth, a tumor on her tummy, arthritis in one shoulder, a flea collar, and no identification."

Being level-headed, the Little Rock people could not wait to get such an animal under their roof.

Although Teasha is a physical mess, her appearance is terrible.

"Because she no longer has teeth to hold it in, her tongue hangs out one side of her mouth, giving her an expression of"—it is a charm difficult to describe.

Yes, they did everything to find the rightful owners.

"We contacted the Humane Society and the Animal Control Center. We read all the LOST ads and took her around to the veterinarians to see if they could identify her."

One look at Teasha, and nobody knew her.

"Unable to locate the owner, we decided to keep her."

It has been a head-leveling experience.

"My check stubs reveal vet bills for nearly $300, which cover tooth extractions, shots, check-ups, license, et cetera."

Those are the check stubs.

"Not included are the costs of food, vitamins, shampoo, special flea dip, toenail clipping, and a $12 sweater that keeps her warm when we take her walking on a chilly evening."

Teasha has only two beds. A day bed in the den and a night bed in the bedroom where she sleeps.

"Unless there is a clap of thunder. In that case she jumps on the bed between us."

Let others be crazy fools.

"Only on half a dozen occasions has my husband run home from work, when I was away from the house and the weather looked like it might be frightening to Teasha."

Teasha goes in the car-car to Razorback game-games.

At Fayetteville she remains in the Holiday Inn, watching television.

"She has spent the night at the Arlington in Hot Springs. Last March she traveled to Dallas for the Southwest Conference basketball tournament."

When the Ozark Folk Center couldn't accommodate Teasha, her level-headed owners canceled reservations and drove to a motel at Mountain View.

It goes on and on.

The point is that our visitor, Mr. Sloan, would be pleased as punch about this people/stray dog relationship. There is no telling who would get punched first.

Dogs Don't Need Baby Talk, Just Get the Phone

She understands completely, Sarah Bennett does, how a reader named "Mr. Sloan" could be fed up with the way people carry on about their dogs.

"There is no better example," Mrs. Bennett writes from Hot Springs, "than the Little Rock couple who take their dog, Teasha, bye-bye in the car-car."

Baby-talking to this dog is absurd.

"By their own admission, Teasha is fifteen years old. If they can't talk to her like an adult by now, there is no hope for Teasha's owners."

Sarah Bennett's dog is six.

"I stopped talking baby-talk to Princess before she was two years old. She has appreciated it more than she can say."

There's one thing that Princess does not appreciate.

"I must hurry along now. It annoys Princess when we don't answer the telephone right away. Makes her a Grumpy Gertie."

The main thing is to use good judgment about pets.

Keep priorities.

Patsy Horton of Little Rock explains, "We have tried to be sensible about our dogs (and cats) and not too sensitive—though we have noticed that friends don't drop in as much as they used to."

Dropping in at the Hortons', you either hold a dog or brace yourself against a wall.

"One of our oldtimers, almost thirteen now, is so happy to see a visitor that he jumps in the visitor's lap and immediately upchucks."

Not all visitors are grateful for so warm a welcome.

Shame on them!

"He is a dear old dog," says Patsy Horton, "and we overlook this annoyance."

It could be that the dog just wants to be sure that the visitor is aware of his presence.

We heard recently about a Little Rock man who attended a large wedding over in Nashville, Tennessee.

The man was a house guest of the bridegroom's parents.

He over-celebrated and late at night found himself wandering in a disoriented state in an upstairs hall of the palatial house.

He found himself by knocking over a small writing desk and sending ink in all directions.

Next morning the guest saw a trail of his own inky handprints on both sides of the hallway, running a considerable length of it.

Unable to face anybody, he quietly departed the house.

So much for the unhappy part. From here on it gets rotten.

Conscience-stricken, the man went back in two weeks bearing candy and flowers for his hostess.

A maid showed him to a large sofa, where he sat uneasily waiting for his hostess.

Uneasily and uncomfortably.

After some minutes the man stood up, turned, and discovered that he had been sitting on a miniature poodle, the hostess's prized pet.

The small creature did not survive the sitting.

This time the wedding guest fled the house in what has been described as absolute horror.

If he ever went back again we have not heard about it.

Tubbs of Harrison, the Cat
Who Came to Dinner

It comes from Paul Darnell of Harrison.

"From time to time I have read in the Arkansas Traveler how animals travel remarkable distances to get back to their homes."

Paul Darnell remembers these heroic stories when he looks out the window into his carport near Harrison.

Sitting out there on top of a freezer is an enormous white cat named Tubbs.

"I don't know what the record is for how far an animal has traveled to get back home. I would say forty miles or so, but in the back of my mind is a cat that traveled on foot from Kansas City to somewhere around Slidell, Louisiana. It could have been the other way around, from south to north. Whichever, that cat had dogged determination."

That cat was not a bucket of lard named Tubbs.

"My purpose is to find out," Darnell says, "what is the shortest distance a cat would have to travel to get back home, and still the cat cannot manage it?"

"Tubbs, you get out of there."

It was a fine spring day eight years ago. Paul Darnell was cleaning crappie in his carport.

"It was the best crappie day I could remember, and I had just acquired a second-hand freezer for the carport."

Getting wind of this event, Tubbs lumbered over from next door to give assistance.

"I don't know if you have ever cleaned fish with one hand while holding off a twenty-pound cat with the other."

It went on for an hour, during which time Paul Darnell got one and a half crappies cleaned.

"Having moved in just a month before, I was determined to be a good neighbor, to both man and man's best friends."

Finally somebody hollered from Tubbs's house next door, "Tubbs, you get away from there! Mr. Darnell did not take you to raise!"

Somebody should have recorded that for evidence.

Here it is in the late spring of 1986, and Paul Darnell looks out the window into his carport, and what does he see resting on top of that freezer with the fish in it but a twenty-pound white cat, a tub of lard.

"Tubbs never made it back home again."

What happened, back there eight years ago, was the telephone rang.

"I was still cleaning on that second crappie, holding Tubbs off with the back of my hand, when the telephone rang. There was no way to leave him out there with the fish, so I picked Mr. Tubbs up, risking severe back injury to myself, and carried him inside."

It was all the hospitality Tubbs needed.

"The distance back to his house is how far I can throw a pinecone, which I did several times those first days, although never with any serious attempt at accuracy."

Tubbs refused to walk away from his job as assistant fish-cleaner.

Eight years later how does a twenty-pound cat get up on top of a freezer?

"When he tells me to, I put him up there."

How does Tubbs get down?

"He tells me, and I get him down."

In the new world, Tubbs eats cat chow and mostly crappie.

Every year or so somebody hollers down from next door, "Tubbs, you get away from there. Mr. Darnell did not take you to raise."

Neither Rain, Snow, nor Owner Can Fool Fido

Eunice Morrison of Conway has a cat who tells her when the postman comes.

The cat is named Fido.

"He sits in the front window and when the postman arrives he comes to wherever I am and stands on my foot."

Fido won't budge until he hears the question, "Did the mail get here?"

Then he leads Eunice Morrison to the front door, looking back over his shoulder to make certain she is following.

This has been going on for seven years.

Two Saturdays ago Fido's owner caught him in his first mistake.

She was in her study room, working on a Sunday school lesson, when the cat came in and stood on her foot.

"What's the matter with you?"

Fido said nothing.

"You know the mail doesn't come on Saturday afternoon."

But he just stood there, both front paws on Eunice Morrison's foot, looking up at her.

"To get rid of him I had to say, 'Did the mail get here?' then go to the front door and act out the motions of looking into the mailbox. Frankly I was feeling disappointed. He had never made a mistake like that before.

In her mailbox Fido's owner found a circular, left by somebody advertising a yard sale down the street.

She went back in and apologized.

Well, the government itself still owes an apology to that dog out on South Brown Street.

We reported this years ago and probably still are not through with it.

But every Wednesday noon when the Civil Defense

siren went off that dog sat down and let out miserable howls. The wailing siren was more than he could bear. He tried to drown it out.

Then there was the Wednesday noon when the siren was broken and didn't go off.

Precisely when it should have, the Brown Street dog sat down and practically yelled his head off. Mystified neighbors said it was so loud, he couldn't have even known it was a solo.

From that day on they looked at the dog with new respect.

For the record, although not wanting to pry, we asked Eunice Morrison how she happened to name her cat Fido.

"I didn't. He was named by my niece, who was then four years old."

Well, maybe that sort of explained it.

"No, it doesn't explain anything. When my niece was four she thought all dogs were boys and all cats were girls."

Persons should learn not to pry into other persons' family names.

Dancing His Dance for Some Other Crowd

What Can Nephew Do with $300?

Our friend Overby inherited some money. Friday he went to the bank and deposited the whole thing, a lump sum of $300.

Overby got the feeling that the bank did not think all that much about it.

"My Uncle Art left it to me," he confided to the teller. The two had done business before, Overby and this teller. He thought of her as a friend.

The teller said, not to Overby but to the next teller over, "Is Glenda still on break?"

The next teller over was giggling into a telephone.

"He was ninety-five," Overby said.

Now both tellers were giggling, sharing what somebody had said on the telephone.

Overby said, "Or he would have been if he had lived until June."

His teller turned to Overby and said, "Sir, did you say you wanted ninety-five dollars?"

Overby said, no, he did not say that.

"I want to put the whole amount in."

We met our friend soon afterward on the street. He wore a wistful expression.

Not that Overby thought $300 was all that much money. His inheritance was not, in fact, $300. It was $280. The people in charge of his uncle's belongings took $20 out for some sort of processing. Overby rounded it out for purposes of discussion.

"My Uncle Art was a good man," he said.

We did not doubt it.

"He worked hard for everything he had. At the end they said he was, well, they said he had only one oar in the water."

Overby didn't know about that, one way or another. He had not talked to his Uncle Art in years.

"I should have got out there to see him, but every time I started something came up."

Uncle Art lived near Mayflower. Also near Greenbrier. And for a time near Beebe. It was always *near* those places. In his own way he farmed.

The man never married.

A note came with Overby's inheritance, a message from the man who had gone on.

"I'm supposed to use the money to buy land," Overby said.

Land?

"Either buy land or put myself through college. Maybe become a teacher."

Overby got out of college in 1955. That was where we met him. He said he was feeling too old to go back through college and become a teacher, especially on $280.

"As for land, I don't know where in the world you could buy anything for two hundred eighty dollars."

Overby is as ignorant when it comes to acreage as the next man.

He said that once years ago his uncle had mentioned a piece of property. A place on Cadron Creek.

"I think it was more in his mind than anyplace else. Anyway it doesn't matter now."

We suggested that the bank might have an idea. Some sort of inheritance counseling service.

Our friend's face turned red.

"I asked about that," he said, looking away up the street. It hadn't been fifteen minutes earlier.

The teller had laughed, saying, "Sir, I wouldn't know what to suggest. Why don't you go over and have a shot at the races?"

Overby wasn't blaming her. Not exactly. Good Lord! Two hundred and eighty dollars!

"With all this amazing interest they're paying, and all these jumbo certificates floating around, I don't suppose a teller with half-sense would even bend over to pick up two hundred eighty dollars if it fell off the counter."

But he was talking about a different kind of money.

On the street Overby smiled. His face recovered a healthy color. He patted his inside coat pocket—"I took it out."

Did what?

"I undeposited the money. It's all right here in my pocket."

Walking from the bank, Overby had been working on a plan. He had some checking to do, but if he could arrange it he was going out to the county farm, where they rent the plots, and get space for a small garden.

He would put in the garden every year, for as long as the money lasted. And while he was out there working in the ground he would think about his Uncle Art.

Caddo Indian Has Message for Visitor

DEGRAY LAKE.–Among the displays here in the Visitors Center, near the dam, you can push a button and listen to a message from a Caddo Indian, a man gone countless moons ago to the Happy Hunting Ground.

Listening to the message, the visitor looks into a glass compartment at a life-sized representation of the voice. The Indian himself. Next to the Caddo is his wife, sitting on the ground, holding a flat, shallow container of grain.

They are dressed forever in their good clothes, raiment of dark animal skins.

With motionless lips the Indian speaks of his surroundings, of these woodlands and waters and skies, of the creatures that inhabit all three.

Take care of these things around you, he says.

Did his wife nod?

Take care of all these things.

"One day you, too, will be gone."

Again we are struck by the Indian's size. Or by the lack of it, the slightness of his frame.

This man in the glass case is not half as big as Victor Mature or Jeff Chandler.

We recall the bones of the Indian found in the Blanchard Springs Cavern. Assembled for display in skeleton fashion, the Blanchard bones could be those of a large child.

How could this be?

Could not the Red Man, the native American, with one hand throw a whole troop of pale-faced pony soldiers over the cliff? He could at the Ritz Theater, on Saturday afternoons in McGehee. And the Red Man never grew tired of it.

That, too, was some moons ago.

Junior Cobb once told us about an Indian graveyard in which the smallest skeleton measured at least—he was reluctant to say it.

"More than six foot six."

That was more like it.

"Some skeletons would be more than seven feet long."

It made no sense that Junior Cobb would exaggerate anything. His life itself was exaggeration.

A woodcarver who lived at Three Brothers, near the Missouri line in Baxter County, Junior flew an airplane the first time he ever got inside one.

Once without special gear he dived deep into Norfork Lake, and Bull Shoals, searching for cherry wood for his carvings. The fishing lures he found down there would have stocked a bait shop.

"I bammed my head"—Junior started laughing, telling about a dive—"I saw this nice piece of cherry and got so eager about it, I swam into a cliff and knocked myself out."

Cobb found the burial ground of giant Indians after reading some markings on a limestone wall.

"I came to the writings as I was riding a horse along the stream. The symbols said that one day's journey up the stream would reach the graves."

Indian directions to themselves.

Junior Cobb made that journey and found no graves.

Then he sat down on some rocks and laughed at himself. Junior Cobb, woodcarver, explorer, student of his own history, natural man—"They didn't ride horseback! They went in canoes!"

So he got a canoe and went back down the stream to the limestone writings, turned around and in the morning began his journey anew.

He found the burial grounds.

"They were tall, those men," Junior said. He paced off the length on an Indian skeleton, then looked without amazement into his listener's eyes.

"I will take you to the burial ground," Junior said, "but you would have to promise never to say where it is."

Take care of these things.

Take care of these things, the Caddo says, dressed here forever in his best of clothes, and beside him his smallish, lovely wife with her display of grain.

This is the way we were during our stay on earth.

Now it is your turn.

"And one day you, too, will be gone."

You Never Know When You'll Need One

BILOXI, Miss.—On page two of the local newspaper, some-body is advertising a hand-held chemical device that will "STOP A 300-POUND MAN IN HIS TRACKS!"

We have sat here by the water most of the day, on the alert, without seeing any 300-pound men. Or any of their tracks, either.

A woman from Michigan was good enough to sit down and explain the whole situation. This woman weighed about 295 pounds.

"They're all over at New Orleans."

The large men?

She shook her head, done up in a Confederate ban-dana. "Don't you see, that's just to show how strong the antichemical is."

She paused to allow us to grasp the meaning of the newspaper advertisement.

Then, "At New Orleans things have gone completely out of hand. People over there are shooting at each other every fifteen minutes."

It didn't matter how much anybody weighed.

"My husband and I, we're not even thinking about going to New Orleans."

The woman shifted in her chair, displacing a ton of sand. She asked where we were from.

Ha! She had lived in Arkansas.

"I was a Ferguson."

Was that so?

"Yes, well, I still am a Ferguson, but now we live in Michigan."

Those Fergusons.

It was in Michigan that she got her own hand-held protection device.

"But still it's not anything like as bad as New Orleans, from everything we hear."

A small tern flew up and contemplated landing on the woman's head. She shooed the bird with her hand, without looking.

In Michigan things were a mile a minute. They were on the go, she and her husband were, all of the time.

"We come down here to get away from people and relax."

Now the small tern was back, ignoring the woman's head and concentrating on her shooing hand. A ring there was the size of a bathroom doorknob. Maybe the tern would like to hatch that.

"Shoo!" the woman says, backhanding at the tern. "These birds are a fool nuisance."

The little tern banks away, taking no real altitude, and slides gently to rest on a damp spit, straightening her shoulders at that precise moment when feet meet sand, walking. No hands, the perfect landing. Without urgency pokes her beak here and there in the wet sand. How many times a day does a bird such as this lift and glide, to land again and poke some more, how much of her life—

"They're a fool nuisance, and they ought to be run off of the beach."

As for Arkansas.

"But, no, we never get back there any more. My husband went back a few Christmases ago, but I have not been inside Arkansas for ten years. Everything is just so much different than it was."

She lived in a house at the bottom of Greers Ferry Lake—"although the water was not there at the time."

She would not begin to know where that house was, not in a month of Sundays.

Now a man came running along the beach, moving laboriously in the sand, a smallish fellow, carrying a camera and yelling her name.

She waved and set up a sideways rocking motion in her chair, over and back three or four times, pulling her feet beneath her, building enough momentum to rise—

"That's my husband."

He walked her to a sign on the beach, something local

to pose by, and with the Gulf of Mexico ignored behind him took her picture against an inland tangle, overgrowth on destruction left more than a decade ago in the assault of Hurricane Camille.

The weathered lettering on the sign said this spot was a refuge of the terns. People should be careful not to disturb the terns or their nesting grounds.

The beach is in decent shape. A bit smudged at the water's edge, but nothing like what you hear from widely-traveled beach experts.

You might want to bring along a hand-held device of some sort, an antichemical, in case you run into any 300-pounders.

A Whompity! Clack-clack!! Dancing Duel

NEW ORLEANS.—This man dancing here in the middle of Bourbon Street, in the middle of the afternoon, has to be in his seventies and there is something unusual about his technique.

Regard the feet.

The shiny light brown shoes whomp down on the pavement, driven by a two-beat rendition of the Notre Dame Fight Song that pours from an open saloon doorway.

But here is the thing about the old street dancer.

It is not until a split-second after his feet land on the pavement, and move on, that one hears the sounds of those feet, whomp, whomp—as though the performance is out of sync.

By this time the old man is into his next movement, interpreting something that nobody has been able to catch up with.

The person not watching this will find it difficult to understand.

The person watching it does not understand it at all.

"That man's a genius," somebody in the street crowd says. "Either that or he's terrible."

We are about to see.

Because just now there lands on the pavement a second cardboard box, not six feet from the old man's collection box—let us see whose feet will bring in the money.

The challenge is thrown down by a youth of no more than fourteen. He is clad in fresh shirt and jeans, and wears new black shoes with huge unscarred taps at the heels and toes.

The youth is muscular. Generations ago he might have been Louis Armstrong.

So the duel begins, not a good tailgate's slide from Preservation Hall, here in the middle of a New Orleans

131

afternoon.

Whomp, (late) whomp.

Clack, clack.

Whompity, whomp!

Clackity, clack-clack!

The ringed crowd thickens and cameras are out.

As for the old man, he is alone in the world. Serene. He is looking everywhere and seeing nothing, dancing his dance for some other crowd.

Not so the youthful walk-on.

He is making freshman mistakes.

But he is giving 110 percent.

Clack, clackity, clack...*"Though the odds be great or small"*...clackity, clackity, clack...*"old Notre Dame will win over all"*...

Never look at your opponent. If he will stare with you, all right. The young can stare down the old.

But now the youth cannot resist cutting his eyes around, at the man who will not acknowledge him. A fatal mistake. Beholding such transport on the old face, the young man revs up to 150 percent, then 170...CLACKITY, CLACKITY...*"shake down the thunder from the sky"*... CLICK-CLACKITY, CLACKITY-CLICK...

(It is a tribute to the Fighting Irish of South Bend that although they did not emerge victorious from the Sugar Bowl game here on January 1, by no means have all their supporters given up and gone home.)

A roar goes up in Bourbon Street. The dancing youth allows himself a faint smile—he cannot help it—and plugs on harder than ever.

But he is wrong. He is through. The duel is over.

Because just now the old man, having come back from wherever he was, has taken his false teeth out, he has only lowers, and has returned them to his mouth backwards.

With the crowd cheering and shutters clicking, the old one finishes the dancing duel solo, whomp, whomp...*"on-ward to vic-tow-ry!"*

A woman standing close to us says to her husband, "This is demeaning."

"It's what?"

"It's embarrassing."

Her husband says, "It sure is. I think he's made a fool out of all of us."

Pausing to Reflect on the Advice of Mr. Kelso

This is the anniversary of the death of Mr. Kelso, who survived repeatedly setting himself on fire, but who could not live with his other habit.

The police wrote up that he was forty. A good, round figure.

"No known address."

We knew Mr. Kelso's address. It was underneath the Cantrell Road overpass, where it crossed above Squatter's Island, by the Arkansas River.

He looked sixty. To boys of twelve, anybody forty appears pretty well used up.

And Mr. Kelso was not exactly normal. He drank breakfast, then ignored the next two meals, spending the day in his living room, which was a big sawdust pile that grew in the shadow of the overpass.

After breakfast, he lay back, head cradled in his hands, the whites of his eyes looking like road maps.

He talked about life.

"There is no such place as the end of your road. You can keep going on. It is all as a man thinketh."

When Mr. Kelso said "thinketh," we were pretty sure he was about 160 years old.

Date of death?

They decided on September 15. It was close enough.

A woman who turned out to be Mr. Kelso's stepsister said he was 34.

She had been afraid of his smoking.

We told her, yes ma'am, we personally had put him out twice. Using sawdust to smother the fire.

Mr. Kelso's stepsister said he was better to her than either one of their fathers.

"He done something terrible. I don't know what it was. But it must have been terrible."

When she passed for old enough to get a job, in a cafeteria on Main Street, Mr. Kelso told her to get her things and move out of the stepfather's house.

Pretty soon afterward he left, too, and never went back there.

They were much younger then.

At their last goodbye, he made her swear that there was no end to her road.

"Swear it!"

She swore it.

On the anniversary of Mr. Kelso's death, in a cardboard house, beneath the Cantrell Road overpass, on or about September 15, 1942—on this anniversary we reaffirm that which he caused us and his stepsister to swear:

"There is no such place as the end of the road."

In Mr. Kelso's honor, we hereby offer proof of what he insisted. Proof gathered from various sources since Mr. Kelso's departure.

First, from Whitney Young, who said it late one night, sitting before a fireplace at Winrock Farm:

"The great challenge facing my people is to manage the interval between where we are now, and where we are going to get."

Whitney Young was black. He described the challenge facing every creature on earth.

Second, the Roman poet Virgil. Sparing us his native language, which she understood well enough to teach, our mother quoted the poet's thought one day as we were crumbling under the weight of some adolescent disaster:

"Perhaps in after years it will delight you to remember these things."

So, manage the interval.

Look back with fondness.

And finally, Winston Churchill.

Undistinguished there as a student, Sir Winston returned to speak at Harrow.

What would this giant of the age say to those who sat where he had sat?

He stood and made this speech:
"Nevah give up.
"Nevah.
"Nevah.
"Nevah!"

*Hearing Things We Never
Heard Before*

What You Hear Is Not What You Get

Somebody has come up with a device to help persons who suffer from ringing ears.

This new thing drowns out the ringing.

We were telling a friend about it.

"Do what?" he said, appearing thoughtful.

"It's a device to help your ear."

He nodded and smiled. "It's nice to have you here, too."

Some persons, getting older, are sensitive about their hearing.

We personally are not disturbed about our hearing. Nearing maturity, we are hearing things we never heard before.

It was mild curiosity that led us to the doctor.

"Describe it," he said. "What does it sound like?"

It was hardly worth talking about.

"Is it like crickets?"

We said actually it was more like wearing windchimes for earrings.

Not that our hearing had been affected. We could still hear snow fall on water.

The doctor sent us into a little room with a specialist. She closed the door and started turning dials.

"Tell me when you hear something."

Hearing snow hit water is one thing. The audiogram is a form of medical trickery.

We advised the specialist that her machines were not working. Not unless they were piping in little windchime recordings.

The doctor looked over these findings. He said:

"How close do you work to the presses?"

Do what?

"The press? Does it roar near your office?"

The last time we heard a press roar was when the

neighborhood drycleaning plant blew up.

"How about loud music?"

We urged the doctor to speak up. Medical schools should stress courses in not mumbling.

"MEW-zik"—his mouth worked in large motions— "Have-you-listened-to-a-lot-of-rock-and-roll?"

Only three teenagers' worth.

It turns out that our phenomenal hearing is the result of social conditions. The noise of living has given us the power to hear windchimes that others cannot even see.

We talked with an older fellow who owns a hearing aid. His family got tired of hollering at him and took up a collection.

You practically can't see the thing in his ear.

"Do what?" he said.

"Your new hearing aid. It's practically invisible."

He said, "I'm not wearing it."

This man has no vanity about him. He would just as soon put an amplified banana in his ear and let others worry about his problem.

But the hearing aid affords more blessings than he can enjoy.

"It means that to hear what I want to hear, I also have to listen to everything else."

In church he could hear bulletins being twisted from four pews away. The slightest snore was audible from nine pews. Congregational coughing sounded like an army tear gas drill.

He leaves his hearing aid at home and trusts the preacher to say the right thing.

There is another thing.

It is our conviction that this man, in his 87th year, can hear anything he wants to.

He can be awakened from an afternoon nod on the couch, an old book in his lap, by the wagging of his dog's tail.

A wagging dog's tail makes the same sound as snow falling on water.

But this man awakens, and smiles at the face that

looks up at him. They go out for a walk in the sun.

What his dog tells him makes more sense than most of the things he hears.

It is about the same with windchimes.

Less-Sleep Proposition Pondered

It is said that the older one gets, the less one has need for sleep.

We cannot vouch for this, having just now moved into our dynamic years. And not all the way at that.

But it is something to think ahead about.

Our older associates insist that the less-sleep proposition is a physical truth.

Professor Mooney shared with a small gathering of friends only this week:

"Before I turned fifty I went to sleep during the ten o'clock news. Now it's all I can do to make it to bed by midnight."

Mrs. Mooney confirmed this.

"Now he goes to sleep during the six o'clock news. At midnight I turn everything out and lead him to bed so he won't hurt himself."

Mrs. Mooney is one to crack a joke.

Our friend Teeter could not have agreed more with the professor.

Teeter remarked that since turning fifty he practically hated sleeping.

"My mind is eager for discovery" is the way he put it.

Teeter spoke of a lively television program he had seen.

"This fellow was explaining the creation of the universe. It all started with a colossal bang"—Teeter separated his hands in the manner of a universe exploding—"and, well, it was just a jim-dandy presentation, the best on the subject I have ever seen."

Mrs. Teeter said actually there were two colossal bangs.

The first was the universe. The second was an ashtray, knocked to the floor by her husband's elbow when he was released abruptly from the paralysis of a massive yawn.

"What was that?" Mrs. Teeter exclaimed, hurrying into the den.

"What was what?" said her husband, his eyes wet with eagerness for discovery.

She led him to bed.

Our friend Simpson, since recently turning fifty, has developed what his wife calls Dunlop's Syndrome.

"His stomach," Mrs. Simpson says, "has dun lopped over his belt."

But this has not altered the man's alertness quotient.

"I'm just as alert as I've ever been," Simpson says.

The other night he sat up and watched the Razorbacks play basketball in Alaska, four time zones away.

"Who won?" his wife said when Simpson reeled into bed.

"Do what?" Simpson said.

So much for the sports news. In truth, Mrs. Simpson had gone in and turned off the test pattern, jabbed her husband in the syndrome with a knitting needle, and returned to bed before the alert one could react.

"It's true," she says. "He's just as alert as he ever was."

Our own indifference to sleep was acquired early.

"Get up, boys. The sun's about to rise."

Our father grew up knowing that anybody caught in bed with the sun shining would never amount to much.

It had been that way around Valley Springs and Bellefont. Get up and do chores. Walk eight miles and spend the day in school. After school, break into a run.

Nowadays we call this jogging. Back then it was known as getting home before dark.

So as a small youth we learned to take sleep or leave it. As a rule, what sleep we left at home, we took at school.

Now our dad is in his 88th year.

His dog is somewhat less old than that.

The man still gets up well before daylight, and insists that his dog do the same thing.

Together they go for a walk, the first half of which the dog manages in a lint-headed stagger.

It is too early to know whether the man will need less

sleep as he goes along.
Or whether the dog will amount to much.

Veteran Comet Viewers Help
Set Stage for Show

It is widely noted that Halley's Comet, the star with the tail, is returning after a journey of three-quarters of a century in space.

Uneducated persons will behold the phenomenon and, swallowed up in their own insignificance, murmur, "What does it mean?"

Sophisticated comet-viewers, on the other hand, will know exactly what to do.

Reading in the October issue of *New Age,* published by the East Arkansas Area Agency on Aging:

"The comet looked like a flame of fire that reached across the sky almost to the ground."

That was 96-year-old Jess Love of Piggott, describing Halley's appearance in 1910.

Mr. Love went on.

"It made a believer out of my neighbor, who used to come in drunk from town every day, but turned to prayer after the comet suddenly appeared."

New Age puts Halley's Comet in interesting perspective.

"The scale of the comet defies imagination."

For example:

"If the comet's icy core were reduced in size to the period at the end of this sentence, the comet would still have a tail of glowing gases over three miles long and 30 feet across, traveling at 244 miles per hour."

That's if Halley's Comet were the size of a period.

"The actual comet has a tail 50 million miles long, 100,000 miles across, and travels at up to 122,000 miles per hour."

This woman told us how it was back in 1910 when Halley's Comet crossed the night sky at Cushman, north of Batesville.

That autumn she turned eleven.

"We went out in the yard several nights. I remember it was warm. Summertime. Or maybe spring. Yes, there was clover in the yard. We kids sat down in the clover."

A crowd gathered in her family's yard.

"The neighbors came because of Mama. Mama wasn't afraid of the comet."

Or maybe she was.

"Daddy was traveling. Whatever Mama thought about the comet, she was not going to let the children be afraid of it."

So those evenings in 1910 the neighbors came over, dragging their cane-bottom chairs, to watch the star with the long tail from the relative safety of the Ramey yard.

"Except for Aunt Seddy. Poor thing."

Aunt Seddy knew the comet's tail was going to drag across Cushman, destroying everything and everybody.

Either that, or the comet would veer from its path and smash into Independence County.

"Who could say? Halley's Comet might even be bigger than the world itself."

So it was a miserable time for Aunt Seddy, those nights out in the yard, shredding a handkerchief in her lap, waiting for the end.

But Halley's Comet passed in the distance. Cushman was not destroyed.

Many persons who saw the comet in 1910 are inspired to rethink personal timetables.

Vada Stubblefield of Pocahontas told an interviewer from *New Age,* the Agency on Aging publication:

"I've always looked forward to seeing the comet again. I figured my time would probably be up if I ever lived to see it return."

Now Halley's is on the way back.

Vada Stubblefield says, "I've decided it's coming back much too soon. I'll have to set another date that I hope to live to see."

145

We had an appointment to see Halley's Comet with a man who watched as a teenager in 1910.

On this replay, he was to provide the expert commentary.

That plan has changed. On September 26, at the age of 91, this man went his own way.

Now we will have to figure it out on our own.

Without half the view he's going to have.

God's Umbrella Covers Even Minds "Prone to Wander"

All his life, which is nine years, Jamie Patterson has wanted to be a preacher.

The youngster was telling his grandfather, J.D. Patterson of Fort Smith, what his first sermon was going to be about.

"It's God's umbrella."

The elder Patterson asked for details.

Jamie said, "That's all there is to it. God has this big umbrella and everybody is protected underneath it. See?"

Granddad Patterson said he saw, and he liked the idea.

"What's your second sermon going to be about?"

The youngster's patience was tried.

"I told you, Granddad. Once you know about the umbrella that's all you need to know."

Patterson said, "But what are you going to tell the folks who come to church the next week?"

Jamie said, "I'm going to say let's all go outside and play baseball."

Our friend Reid is worried because his mind wanders in church.

It comes with no warning.

The preacher can be up there reading from Philippians.

Or giving an important announcement.

Or blessing the collection plates.

Reid's mind gets up and eases out of the pew. Turns up the aisle. Heads out the door. His mind disappears down the street, with no more Christian sense of direction than a dried-up oak leaf lurching through an October neighborhood.

Worried is not quite the word for it.

Reid knows he can't sneak this thing past the Lord,

any more than you can sneak sunrise past a rooster.

Reid told us that if a wandering mind is a sin, he just hopes to hell it's not one of the Big Ones.

Reid's mind has been wandering in church (wandering out of church) since his feet stuck straight out in the pew.

Back when he thought Philippians were The Philippinos.

"Good work!"

Those words were written on a piece of paper by the giant of a man who sat beside young Reid every Sunday morning.

The words judged some crayon work in Reid's lap.

Do you think it was the Lord's business? The Baby Jesus? Some lambs?

The crayon work was, in fact, a black haystack with a red faucet angling out at the top.

Young Reid's version of a Thanksgiving turkey.

Years later, many years, he found that work, on the day the family buried the giant. He turned out to be five feet, nine inches.

Reid's mind wandered wildly through the funeral service.

He was running to catch up with his father. One last time. To say to him, "Good work."

In his worst moments, Reid fears detection.

He gets the idea that a cartoon balloon appears above his head, and everybody in church can read his vagrant thoughts.

Reid becomes so convinced of this, he stands invisible in the aisle and looks into the pew at himself, fingers laced between his knees, mouth slightly open.

This division lasts only a second before Reid is reunited with himself, swallowing a dry swallow, looking around to determine whether anybody else saw his mind return.

But that is not the detection Reid fears most.

"A good preacher has the hardest job in the world," Reid said. "Do you want me to tell you why?"

We were drifting in the middle of Lake Ouachita. The alternative to hearing was to go over the side.

"I am *aware* of God!" Reid's statement cracked the air, cracked it and then rolled out across the lake's surface in all directions.

We considered going over into ninety feet of water.

"A preacher's problem," Reid said, "is he has to spend ninety percent of his pulpit time trying to raise the congregation's awareness level."

Reid said he already was aware of God, not booming it this time, not scaring the fish, and moreover God was aware of his awareness.

"But the preacher, bless his heart, he has to keep coming after it, keep coming every Sunday, until if you're already aware of God it begins to sound like the marching band at halftime, when all the musicians turn away from the field microphone except the trombones. I mean, it's strong, but the song is more beautiful than that."

It made Reid's mind wander.

"Sometimes I have the urge to go up there and get the preacher by the elbow and whisper to him, 'Let's get out of here.'"

We asked Reid why he was telling us all of this.

Our friend had put his casting rod down. His hands were laced between his knees, his mouth slightly open.

"Telling you all what?" he said.

He is a man in trouble.

And not getting any younger.

One Was Missing at Christmastime

Where the old woman sat, at the end of the sofa, the light from the end table lamp spilled into her lap, leaving her face suspended in early evening darkness, like a witness testifying anonymously.

She caught the lamplight in her palms. Hands turned up from the wrists, momentarily abandoned.

Then the hands got busy again.

"I can't get these cleaned." The old woman rubbed at her eyeglasses.

He answered that cataracts were not removed with the hem of a smock.

The old woman's son, an old person himself, had a disrespectful mouth.

She snorted at him and rubbed.

They sat, and at last they allowed it to come.

Wreath of cones. Red candles and white. A basket of cards. This music.

Merely the hopes and fears of all the years.

It was coming, all right. Who could stop it?

"Sixty-three." She set her hands aside again.

The son urged a different direction, reminding her that she was terrible in arithmetic.

Of course she ignored him.

"Do you realize this will be the first Christmas in sixty-four years your daddy and I haven't been together?"

The son said did she realize he had never spent a Christmas without him.

He knew that sitting there in the dark, her head above the lamplight, she was trying to figure out which was longer.

Soon her hands were busy again. She said, "I suppose so."

These days the old woman needed that dark above the lamplight to carry around with her. Something to hide her head in.

Because there was no telling where it would happen next. Or why.

At the grocery store, writing her check, she asked the clerk to repeat the cash register total.

"Ma'am, it's forty-two eighty."

They shot into her eyes. Tears just bursting. Alarming the clerk.

That was not enough—"forty-two eighty"—not for all their groceries, for the prescriptions, for the gear that little babies and old men wear, for the "little something" he would hide his eyes for when she got back home and took it slowly from the sack.

What the old woman wouldn't give to have their grocery bill back.

So it was settled, then, about Christmas morning.

"I'd like to take five roses out there. One for each of you children, and one for me and one for Buddy."

At her feet, in the spill of lamplight, the dog heard his name and raised his head. Seeing that it would amount to nothing, he went back to sleep.

She said, "Have you heard that many flowers get stolen from cemeteries?"

He had not heard. Except, well—there was Julia Cordelia's son. When George was a little boy, on the way home from school, nearly every afternoon he stopped by the cemetery and picked out something nice for his mother. A thoughtful child.

About the roses on Christmas morning. The old son said, yes, he would drive her out there.

But he had a theory about that.

When she did not ask what his theory was, he spoke it anyway.

It was his theory that people who took flowers to the cemetery went out there because of some sort of unfinished business.

They sat and let it come.

As it got late, she stood and took an envelope from her smock pocket.

151

It was for the son. His Christmas present.

Passing on her way to bed, she put the envelope in his hands.

On the outside, her handwriting did a little something to Santa's language.

"Merry Christmas. Ha! Ha! Ha!"

Not bad for an old blind woman without a husband.

Merry Christmas, Mom.

Somebody Will Forgive a Father's Gulping

Young Radioman on *Caron* To Be Awhile Longer

The inquiry comes from Pete and Phyllis Cathcart, retired Navy people living at Greers Ferry Lake.

"Late last summer you went to Norfolk, Virginia, to say goodbye to a young radioman who was leaving for the Mediterranean on the destroyer *Caron*.

"You said you would meet again when the leaf turned green.

"At our house the leaf is turning green. Is there news to be shared?"

The news is the man from Libya rode out in his patrol boat and drew a line in the water and said, "This is the Line of Death."

The radioman, gone six months now, writes home that you can't see that line in the water, but you can feel it.

He will be awhile longer.

Watching for the Morning
with Dogs, U-Haul, Rain

NORFOLK, Va.—On the motel parking lot, Mr. Sparling stands in first light, guarding his trailer load of furniture, hunch-shouldered with a raindrop on his nose.

The morning sky is in tatters, dark shreds flung low across Chesapeake Bay into southern Virginia. A moment ago tires whined along Military Highway. Now on this wet surface the big rigs hiss.

Mr. Sparling is not a happy man.

"I am Mr. Sparling," he said, not unclasping his arms. "From South Carolina."

By way of response we recalled, for some reason, that a thief took a raincoat from our car at Spartanburg. It was years ago.

Mr. Sparling sniffed that he was not that thief.

"Although I could use a raincoat now."

He squinted at his wristwatch, again without unclasping his arms, and wondered when Mrs. Sparling would decide to wake up.

"I should have got a room for only one person."

They had come in the night before, a long pull up through North Carolina, and when the desk clerk said how many in your party, Mr. Sparling, of course, said, "Two."

But then, tired as he was, he could not close his eyes for worrying about the furniture.

"This is every last stick of it."

The Sparlings were moving to Carlisle, Pennsylvania.

On there somewhere with every last stick of furniture were Mr. Sparling's bottom teeth. At least the teeth were not in his mouth. At doleful intervals, the lower part of his face collapsed inward with a sigh.

Mr. Sparling was not somebody's idiot. He knew that in a city such as Norfolk, Virginia, home of the world's largest naval base, there was going to be a certain amount of mischief.

Without so much as one wink of sleep, he got up and dressed and came outside to guard the furniture.

Since 10:15 last night, Mrs. Sparling had been alone in Room 141, sleeping at the rate of two persons.

"I could have saved eight dollars," Mr. Sparling said, his lower face falling inward.

Now here are two large wet dogs, brown and browner, each more unappealing than the other, both smelling like what they are, and with no attitudes of remorse.

Unappealing except for their eyes. The dogs' eyes are ghastly yellow, brimming with exploratory friendship.

And they are in curious postures.

These dogs are standing sideways to Mr. Sparling, bent into dog semicircles so that their heads and tails are closer to him than their middles. They are looking for approval, a pat on one end or the other, at the same time guarding against one more of what must have been 1,000 rejections.

Mr. Sparling, his morning in disarray, is 1,001.

"What are you looking at?" he demands of the dogs.

They step slightly away, heads lowering, tails wagging somewhat faster.

Beneath the trailer, looking out, their eyes lose nothing in the way of yellow or in the way of friendship.

It seems to us that Mr. Sparling from South Carolina has earned a verbal poke.

We tell him, really, he should have more faith.

God has to be up all night anyway.

Had he turned this furniture guarding over to God, he could have spent the night in 141, along with Mrs. Sparling, lowering the per capita cost of a night's sleep.

Mr. Sparling asks us, in the tone used for asking dogs what they are looking at, "If God is taking care of everything, why are you standing out here before daylight in the rain?"

Later we watch from our window as he feeds the yellow-eyed dogs peanut butter crackers bought from the machine.

This water here in the Chesapeake Bay, it touches water that touches water that touches the waters of the Persian Gulf.

What we are doing is, we are saying one more goodbye to a radioman aboard the naval destroyer *Caron*.

Awaiting Arrival of One Big, Fast Floating Object

NORFOLK, Va.—Other than being longer than a football field and faster than a racehorse, the naval destroyer *Caron* is pretty much your average floating object.

Perhaps there is another difference or two.

This spring, when the United States Sixth Fleet demonstrated the right of innocent passage, it sent *Caron,* in the company of the cruiser *Yorktown,* deep into the Black Sea, to within six miles of the Russian coast.

The weekly news magazine *Time* put it this way:

"Caron is an intelligence-gathering ship capable of searching out newly established radar installations."

The Soviet Union would not think of doing such a thing itself. Not unless it was off the coast of Florida or Hawaii. At the sight of *Caron* and *Yorktown,* Mother Russia hurried out onto her porch at Sevastopol, to twist her apron and point her finger.

The Navy vessels departed, with no more than a goodwill gesture or two.

There is another thing about *Caron.*

To show Libya that it does not own international waters, the United States sent three warships across Col. Moammar Khadafy's "Line of Death." With *Caron* the spearpoint, these ships steamed three days in the Gulf of Sidra.

Colonel Khadafy did not shake his finger. He sent missiles.

It is a matter of military history that those missiles were prayed into the water by a Navy dad back at Little Rock, Arkansas.

Which brings us to the real difference between *Caron* and other floating objects.

On board is a youngster, a radioman, who has been disobeying his father.

If we told this child once, we told him a thousand

times. Son, play in your own yard.

It is a cold gray morning on Chesapeake Bay, 48 degrees and blowing rain. The sky and the water are the color of battleships.

At DESRON 10 (for Destroyer Squadron) they told us *Caron* would arrive at "Yankee" buoy at 0940 hours, which is 9:40 a.m.

"Sir, Yankee buoy is the thirty-minute mark."

Then she would be gathered up—*Caron* would be—by a small harbor craft, and the destroyer would come home again, after 230 days at sea, touching the pier at 1010 hours.

To provide a time cushion, we came to Norfolk Naval Station a bit early, five hours actually, arriving at first light.

It took an hour to get a pass.

We are parked at Pier 7. In the driver-side window appears a youthful face under a working man's baseball cap, black with gold lettering—"USS YELLOWSTONE."

"Sir, they are going to be on you faster than stink on a skunk."

Stink on a skunk?

"Security, sir. For sure with that camera."

We have uncased the 35-millimeter camera, to focus on the hull numbers of the nuclear cruiser *Virginia,* docked at Pier 7, the host ship for families meeting *Caron.*

"Sir, it's the terrorist threats. Security is tight. If I were you I would not wave that camera around. I would not act in a nervous manner."

You may ask yourself this question:

On a morning when six warships are returning home from the Mediterranean, midst a hail of terroristic threats, with security tightening down around the world, you may ask yourself—on such a morning in Norfolk how long does it take stink to get on a skunk?

But there is no time to answer.

Even as he offers advice, the young man in the Yellowstone ballcap dematerializes and is replaced in the car

159

window by a policeman holding a two-way radio near his mouth.

"Sir, state your purpose here."

We state that we are meeting the *Caron*, a destroyer longer than a racehorse and faster than a football field.

"Show me your identification."

From a container of cards, we hand over something good for cashing checks at Safeway in 1981.

Mrs. Caron Won't Meet Her Son, Will Greet a Ship

NORFOLK, Va.—On the forward deck of the nuclear cruiser *Virginia,* moored at the largest naval base in the free world, a young sailor points and describes how it will happen.

"Sir, you will first spot the *Caron* steaming around the tip of that carrier there."

She left in August, *Caron* did, under a hot and copper sky. After 230 days she returns to safe anchorage on a cold, gray morning in April.

But not cold and gray for families waiting on *Virginia's* deck.

Aboard the inbound destroyer are some 320 officers and men. Since leaving Norfolk, they have been around.

In his final message before leaving the Mediterranean, *Caron's* commanding officer wrote to families:

"Your Caronman is coming home from the sea. He has probably changed a little since you last saw him. Since then he has performed in a superlative manner, he has answered his country's call and is a veteran of action against an enemy of the United States of America. He is a diplomat, a surface warrior, and a peacekeeper in a troubled world. Treat him like the hero he is, he deserves the recognition.

"Your shipmate, Lou Harlow."

Forty percent of those on *Caron* are under 25.

Steady on the deck. You will spot nothing out there if your eyes fill up with salt water.

We are grateful to the reader for allowing us to get this particular ship home.

Many ships have sailed. Many more will follow. God bless them all. But last August we told a young radioman that we would see him here again when the leaf turned green. Since that time we have been paddling as hard as we could, trying to keep up, down to the Caribbean, out across the Atlantic, into the Mediterranean, up through the Black Sea, down into the Gulf of Sidra, across the so-called "Line of Death."

It has been exhausting work. Now on *Virginia's* deck, light-headedness is taking control of the whole thing.

"Hello. I'm Mrs. Caron."

She is standing squarely in front of us, a woman in— what?—her sixties, the pleasant voice jerking us back from the far reaches of Chesapeake Bay.

Mrs. Caron? Of course you are. Joining the frivolity, we tell her, sure, and we are "Mr. Caron," and isn't it a beautiful morning!

She says nothing, but goes on smiling, an even, beautiful smile, this woman ignoring our lightheadedness, gracefully allowing something to sink in.

So it is the truth. She is his mother.

Wayne Caron was 21 years old.

Out of high school, he had enlisted in the Navy at Boston. It was the summer of 1966.

After boot camp, he trained for medical service.

July 28, 1968, Hospital Corpsman Third Class Wayne Maurice Caron was platoon corpsman with a Marine company sweeping through an open rice field in Quang Nam Province, Vietnam.

The description accompanied his Medal of Honor:

"Petty Officer Caron's unit started receiving enemy small-arms fire. Upon seeing two Marine casualties fall, he immediately ran forward to render first aid, but found that they were dead. At this time the platoon was taken under intense small-arms and automatic weapons fire. As he moved to aid wounded comrades, Petty Officer Caron was hit in the arm by enemy fire. Although knocked to the ground, he regained his feet and continued to aid the injured Marines."

Again young Caron was struck, this time in the leg.

"Nonetheless, he crawled the remaining distance and provided medical aid to a severely wounded man."

Now for a third time he was struck by enemy fire.

"Courageously and with unbelievable determination, he continued his attempt to reach a third Marine until he himself was killed by an enemy rocket."

Janet Caron will not meet her son this day in Norfolk. She has come to welcome the ship that honors Wayne Caron's name, and be honored by it.

Family by Family, Sailors of *Caron* Are Reunited

NORFOLK, Va.—Oh! It was something to behold, all right.

Harbor horns wailed.

Seagulls shrieked.

On the pier a high school band flogged "Anchors Aweigh."

When after 230 days the destroyer *Caron* came home again, her decks lined shoulder-to-shoulder with sailors dressed in blue—well, at the sight of that, otherwise strong adults broke down and wept.

Even some of the woman cried.

Being a professional observer, we took the whole thing in stride.

Security clearance came despite our personal identification, which features the lopheaded photograph found on Arkansas driver's licenses and in post office lobbies.

Nobody in his right mind would show such a thing, and in times of terrorism security experts are looking for persons not in their right minds.

"Just be careful what pictures you take," a guard said finally.

We chose an aperture setting of f5.6, alternating shutter speeds between 1/60th and 1/100th, and, as instructed, carefully took 36 pictures of the inside of our lens cap.

There will be plenty of copies to go around.

First to the red carpet unrolled at the foot of the gangplank was Janet Caron, mother of the hospital corpsman for whom the warship is named.

His father, Joseph Caron, wore the baseball cap, black with gold letting: "USS CARON DD-970."

"This is our family," Joe Caron said, watching the destroyer draw near.

When the parents learned that the Navy might name a ship for their son, Wayne Caron, there was a time of anxiety.

Joe Caron of Massachusetts says, "We thought, what if it gets assigned to the West Coast? How would we ever get to see it?"

Mrs. Caron sat down and wrote a letter to the Navy.

In October 1977, nine years after Wayne Caron died in a Vietnamese rice paddy, winning the Medal of Honor, the ship bearing his name was commissioned and given a permanent home at Norfolk.

"I don't have to tell you," Joseph Caron said to another father on the pier, "what this means to us."

So it was that families went aboard *Caron.*

Following Janet Caron across the red carpet, up the steps and along the gangplank—young persons and old persons, black persons and white persons, quiet and loud persons, nervous, laughing and crying, looking for the right set of dress blues.

A child on her mother's shoulder blinked in alarm.

"She was four months old when her daddy left. He's not going to believe this. I'm not sure I believe it, either."

One by one, they search and find. Family by family. Search and find, and reunite.

In what is called the mess deck, *Caron* is serving coffee and sweet rolls. The noise level grows, more people arriving, emotions tumbling in.

The child who had been four months old now is in the arms of a young man in dress blues. She studies his face with her head drawn back, eyes blinking faster than ever.

As families went aboard, we kept to the pier, and first saw him high up there, leaning on a rail, identical blue uniforms at each shoulder, sailors looking down, each trying to sort somebody out of the crowd.

That young face, a long time gone, seemed thinner.

He explained why an hour later, on shore, at lunch.

"The last month or so, nobody on ship has eaten anything. They say it just happens. You lose your appetite."

And now?

"Thanks for the offer, but I'm just not hungry. Oh, I'll try to eat a little something."

The little something is a platter that goes for nineteen dollars.

It's the sort of effort that makes a dad proud.

The *Caron* Certainly Not the Good Ship Lollipop

NORFOLK, Va.—The scuttlebutt is that in a fierce mock sea battle, all but six of thirty-two warships have gone down.

This was preparatory to crossing the Atlantic.

The unofficial report goes further that among the six surviving vessels was DD-970. The destroyer *Caron.*

When you have driven 1,000 miles to say goodbye to a *Caron* radioman, it is good to see him coming along the pier, undestroyed.

Now get some really good news, conveyed with high enthusiasm by one of the radioman's cronies, himself on the order of 24 years of age:

"Did you hear it? We're going to draw combat pay!"

How much rejoicing can a dad's heart stand?

It is not the Good Ship Lollipop.

In length, the specifications read, Caron is 563 feet and 4 inches.

We have been aboard, more than a year ago, but even now nothing prepares us for that figure.

Certainly not the dictionary:

"De-stroy-er, n. A fast, relatively small warship armed mainly with five-inch guns, originally designed to destroy torpedo boats, now used as an escort in convoys, in anti-submarine duties, etc."

Not specified is the meaning of "etc."

Here is a *thing* measuring just thirteen yards short of two football fields, cutting through the water at speeds that would get *Caron* arrested on most Little Rock streets.

"Four main propulsion gas turbines produce more than 20,000 horsepower each to drive the ship at speeds in excess of 30 knots."

Thirty knots plus. That's the closest they'll say. They add a wink.

Somebody will forgive a father's gulping.

Only a year or so ago, not much more than that, the radioman was capsizing unsinkable toys in his bathtub. The toys were sinking.

Regard what is preparing to cross the Atlantic again:

"The armament aboard *Caron* consists of two Mark 45 lightweight five-inch guns, two Mark 15 Close-In Weapon Systems, anti-submarine rocket (ASROC) launcher, torpedo tubes, and helicopters for ASW detection and long-range weapons delivery."

Please be patient.

"The Mark 45 gun is fully automatic, electronically controlled, and can fire a projectile over ten miles at the rate of 20 rounds per minute. The Mark 15 Vulcan Phalanx 'Gatling Gun' is also fully automatic and can fire 3,000 rounds per minute.

"*Caron* is also fitted with the HARPOON surface-to-surface cruise missile and the NATO Sea Sparrow missile for defense against missiles and aircraft."

Now here is a crony, maybe a bit saltier, maybe even 25 years old. Rojo Grande, he is called. Big Red, for how he looks.

"Mr. Allbright, I don't know what Paul has told you."

Not much. He talked more as new man in the radio shack. As a petty officer, with seven months to go, he does not say much.

Rojo confides, "Mr. Allbright, it's awful what we can do, if we have to."

And what the other side can do, whoever that is, it's awful, too.

Incredible déjà vu.

Plane trails crossing in a high, hot sky.

Morning coming down on the world's largest naval base.

Now, a final time, there is no gate pass.

No civilian passing beyond this gate.

"Well, Dad. Goodbye."

Goodbye.

"Thanks for coming."

Thanks? All right.

"I'll see you."

I will see you when the leaf turns green.

The radioman is gone.

Goodbye.

Goodbye, and thanks again for having been a little boy.

Because whatever that was, it's over. And it won't be back again.

CHARLES ALLBRIGHT has been a reporter, editorial writer, and columnist for the *Arkansas Gazette* since 1955, except for seven years spent as a speechwriter for Governor Winthrop Rockefeller. He has written the *Gazette's* "Arkansas Traveler" column continuously since 1974.